Theos – clear thinking on religion

Theos is the UK's leading religion and society think tank. With our ideas a combined circulation of 160 million in the past 5 years, we are shaping the debate about the role of faith in contemporary society by means of high quality research, events and media commentary. We provide a credible, informed and gracious Christian voice in our mainstream public conversations.

The *Economist* calls us "an organisation that demands attention", and Julian Baggini, the influential atheist philosopher, has said "Theos provides rare proof that theology can be interesting and relevant even – perhaps especially – for those who do not believe."

To learn more, check us out on social media:

twitter.com/theosthinktank | facebook.com/theosthinktank | www.theosthinktank.co.uk

Why we exist

Religion has emerged as one of the key public issues of the 21st century, both nationally and globally. Our increasingly religiously-diverse society demands that we grapple with religion as a significant force in public life. Unfortunately, much of the debate about the role and place of religion has been unnecessarily emotive and ill-informed. We exist to change that.

We reject the notion of any possible 'neutral' perspective on these issues. We also reject the idea that religion is a purely private matter or that it is possible to divide public and private values for anyone.

We seek, rather, to recognise and analyse the ethical ideas and commitments that underlie public life and to engage in open and honest public debate, bringing the tradition of Christian social and political thought to bear on current issues. We believe that the mainstream Christian tradition has much to offer for a flourishing society.

What we do

Theos conducts research, publishes reports, and holds debates, seminars and lectures on the intersection of religion, politics and society in the contemporary world. We also provide regular comment for print and broadcast media and briefing and analysis to parliamentarians and policy makers. To date, Theos has produced over 50 research reports focusing on the big issues impacting British society, including welfare (*The Future of Welfare: A Theos Collection*), law (*"Speaking Up" – Defending and Delivering Access to Justice Today*), economics (*Just Money: How Catholic Social Teaching can Redeem Capitalism*), multiculturalism (*Making Multiculturalism Work*) and voting reform (*Counting on Reform*), as well as on a range of other religious, legal, political and social issues.

In addition to our independently-driven work, Theos provides research, analysis and advice to individuals and organisations across the private, public and not-for-profit sectors. Our staff and consultants have strong public affairs experience, an excellent research track record and a high level of theological literacy. We are practised in research, analysis, debate, and media relations.

Where we sit

We are committed to the traditional creeds of the Christian faith and draw on social and political thought from a wide range of theological traditions. We also work with many non-Christian and non-religious individuals and organisations.

Theos was launched with the support of the Archbishop of Canterbury and the Cardinal Archbishop of Westminster, but it is independent of any particular denomination. We are an ecumenical Christian organisation, committed to the belief that religion in general and Christianity in particular has much to offer for the common good of society as a whole. We are not aligned with any point on the party political spectrum, believing that Christian social and political thought cuts across these distinctions.

Join the discussion by becoming a Friend of Theos

Impact how society views Christianity and shape the cultural debate

The Friends' Programme is designed specifically for people who wish to enter the heart of the current debate. When you join, our commitment is to keep you informed, equipped, encouraged and inspired so that you can be a voice in the public square with us.

As a member of the Friends' Programme, you are provided with:

- *Hard copies of all our latest reports* on the most pressing issues – social justice, welfare, politics, spirituality, education, money, atheism, humanism…
- *Free access to our events.* Theos hosts a number of high calibre speakers (e.g. Rowan Williams, Larry Siedentop, Grace Davie) and debates ('Magna Carta and the future of liberty', 'Does humanism need Christianity?'). As a friend, you will receive invitations to all these without charge.
- *A network of like-minded people* who wish to share ideas and collaborate with one another. We host networking events which help you meet fellow Friends and build your own network, allowing ideas to flow and connections to form.
- *Our monthly e-newsletter* which is your one-stop digest for the latest news regarding religion and society.
- **If you join as an Associate**, you are *invited to private functions with the team*, allowing you to discuss upcoming projects, review the latest issues and trends in society, and have your say in where you see the public debate is going.

You can become a Friend or Associate today by visiting our website
www.theosthinktank.co.uk

If you'd prefer additional information, you can write to us directly:
Friends Programme, Theos, 77 Great Peter Street, London, SW1P 2EZ

If you have any inquiries regarding the Programme, you can email us at:
friends@theosthinktank.co.uk

Catholic Social Thought and Catholic Charities in Britain Today: Need and Opportunity

Published by Theos in 2016
© Theos

ISBN 978-0-9931969-3-5

Some rights reserved – see copyright licence for details
For further information and subscription details please contact:

Theos
Licence Department
77 Great Peter Street
London
SW1P 2EZ

T 020 7828 7777
E hello@theosthinktank.co.uk
www.theosthinktank.co.uk

contents

acknowledgement — 6

foreword — 7

executive summary — 8

introduction — 16

chapter 1:   CST in practice — 23

chapter 2:   being Catholic today — 49

chapter 3:   the challenges facing Catholic charities — 58

conclusion — 69

acknowledgements

Theos would like to thank the Charles Plater Trust, and Kevin Ambrose in particular, for their generous support both in commissioning this project and in their recognition of the importance of Catholic Social Teaching as it relates to the Catholic charitable sector.

The project as a whole would not have been possible without the support of our six partner charities; the Apostleship of the Sea, Caritas Birmingham, Father Hudson's Care, Retrouvaille England and Wales, the SVP and Worldwide Marriage Encounter. It was their willingness to provide interviewees and to serve as case studies for the research that has made the project a success.

Dr James Hanvey SJ and Nick Townsend provided immensely helpful feedback and advice in preparing the final report and we are grateful to His Eminence Cardinal Vincent Nichols for providing the foreword and to Edmund Adamus from the Diocese of Westminster and the staff at CSAN for their advice and help in identifying partner charities.

Particular thanks are also due to Hannah Malcolm and Gillian Madden for their help in completing the interviews for this project, and Clare Purtill for all her work in preparing the final briefing documents.

foreword

This report by Theos on *Catholic Social Thought and Catholic charities in Britain Today*, commissioned and supported by the Charles Plater Trust, brings into sharp focus the broken and wounded world in which we live and how Catholic charities are called to imitate Christ in their work with the vulnerable and marginalised.

I express my warmest thanks to Theos, for their theoretical research on Catholic Social Teaching, their research on the six charities, the interviews undertaken and most especially for presenting the results of the analysis in a clear and coherent fashion. By studying the relationship between Catholic Social Teaching and those Catholic charities, the author of the report presents an ideal opportunity to reflect on how this relationship can be developed for the mutual benefit of all. As the Executive Summary concludes: "Catholic Charities represent a remarkable asset for the Catholic Church and wider society, but more needs to be done to recognise and support that work."

With my thanks too to the Charles Plater Trust for funding this important project.

✠ H.E. Cardinal Vincent Nichols
Archbishop of Westminster

executive summary

why this project?

Catholic Social Teaching (CST) is receiving significant public attention as part of the public debate on the future of politics and economics. Less attention has been paid to the extent to which Catholics are themselves embodying CST to improve their local communities. In particular the Catholic charitable sector offers a case study of how these principles can be enacted in practice. The purpose of this project has been to explore Catholic charities, the extent to which they understand and embody CST, what it means to be a Catholic charity in Britain today and the challenges (both practical and theoretical) facing them in their work. It argues that Catholic charities represent a remarkable asset for the Catholic Church and wider society, but that more needs to be done to recognise and support their work.

Catholic charities

The Catholic charitable sector in Britain represents a hugely diverse range of activities. Aside from parishes, dioceses and religious orders there are also Catholic schools, universities, colleges, and social action work in every conceivable area.

There is a live question of what really counts as a Catholic charity. The Church insists charities using the name "Catholic" have a license from their local bishop to do so.[1] However, there are a great many charities that, for one reason or another, do not choose or are ineligible to be called Catholic, but that continue to claim a Catholic inspiration for their work. In addition there is a significant quantity of charitable work which does not come under the umbrella of a registered charity but instead involves activity (perhaps within a parish setting) that goes under the radar.

Given the sheer breadth of activity it would be impossible to provide a comprehensive study of the sector as a whole. Instead this research relies on very different Catholic charities.

- The Apostleship of the Sea (AoS) works to support seafarers in Britain's ports. It provides chaplaincy and ship visiting services to all of Britain's ports. It is an agency of the Catholic Bishops' Conferences of England and Wales and Scotland.

- Caritas Archdiocese of Birmingham is a network for Catholic social action work in the Birmingham Archdiocese set up by Archbishop Longley in October 2014. It is also the smallest of our charities, and the only one that is not a registered charity.

- Father Hudson's Care (FHC) functions as the social care agency for the Archdiocese of Birmingham. FHC was founded in 1902 to look after homeless Catholic children. Today it works in a wide range of social care work, including with adults with disabilities, schools, fostering, the elderly and a range of community based projects.

- Retrouvaille is a marriage crisis charity that works to help couples with serious marital difficulties. It started in Canada in the 1970s. Retrouvaille works closely with marriage and family life officers in dioceses but is not listed as a Catholic charity on the Charity Commission website.

- The Saint Vincent de Paul Society (SVP) is one of Britain's largest and best known Catholic charities. It has around 8,000 members who work on a range of social action work, but is best known for visiting individuals and families. It is also the oldest of our charities, having operated in England and Wales since 1844 and internationally since 1833.

- Worldwide Marriage Encounter (WWME) is a marriage charity whose primary focus is on enriching and refreshing the relationships of couples who are engaged, married, or in long-standing relationships. It also does work with couples preparing for marriage.

findings

1. CST in practice

Our research identified six key themes of CST within the charities we studied. Five of these (the option for the poor, solidarity, subsidiarity, personalism and family) we had broadly anticipated to find. The sixth, evangelisation, was less expected but arose in a number of different interviews and charities.

Of these themes, the option for the poor and solidarity (along with other ideas from CST like the common good and human dignity) were terms and ideas that arose regularly in interviews without prompting, though the degree to which they were really understood varied significantly. Other principles, notably subsidiarity, were often evident in practice, but were not terms that were used or at least understood except by a minority of interviewees.

1. option for the poor

The language of taking the option for the poor was much in evidence across our charities. There was a conscious desire to move the idea of poverty beyond material need. Accordingly, several charities put a particular focus on countering relational poverty – that is isolation due to age, language, employment etc. Similarly there was a strong emphasis on the call to the margins – to be there for people on the edge of society. The focus on spiritual needs varied significantly across charities, but was a critical element in a few.

2. solidarity

Terms like "solidarity" and "common good" were frequently used by interviewees, but not always well understood. The common good and the idea of being neighbourly were, however, discussed at length in terms of Catholic responsibility to the local area. Solidarity was necessarily kept in tension with a need to be careful with funds to guarantee sustainability. That tension was unpopular with some interviewees who wanted charities to spend more of their assets. The need to raise the profile of the charities and speak up for the voiceless was a growing concern across the sector, but one which was proving especially difficult to accomplish.

3. subsidiarity

"Subsidiarity" was not a well understood term – suggesting the Church has more to do in providing education on this CST principle. There were exceptions to this general rule – particularly among charity trustees, and despite "subsidiarity" as a term rarely being used in interviews there was a strong theme of the importance of finding local solutions to local problems. Networks and umbrella charities had a significant role to play in resourcing and supporting smaller charities and projects, particularly on time-consuming or technical things like legal work, accounting and safeguarding procedures.

4. personalism

"Personalism" works as a meta-theme covering a number of important CST principles. At its most basic it is the idea that humans are necessarily inter-connected and cannot be seen simply as atomised individuals. Despite the importance placed on personalism in the work of John Paul II the term has made little meaningful impact in forming the understanding of CST among British Catholics. That said, the commitment to human dignity was consistently prized as a critical aspect of the work of Catholic charities – and as a differentiating factor from other public service providers.

Likewise the importance of Catholic charities in having a real and actual presence in people's lives and establishing personal relationships was well-established throughout the charities. Tied closely to the idea of personal presence was a recognition that that came with the need to embody true "com-passion" – i.e. more than sympathy but actually suffering alongside people. This comes with something of a health warning – as one interviewee made clear "it hurts more that's the truth. When someone dies or goes off the rails it hurts that much more because you actually knew them".

5. family

Whether directly or indirectly there was a clear focus across the charities on supporting families. In particular there was a widespread recognition that people are never simply individuals, any action will have an indirect impact on family and ultimately broader society.

6. evangelisation

None of our case study charities wanted to engage in "proselytism". There was, however, remarkable evidence for the role charities played in growing Catholics. The growth in spirituality among people who had already considered themselves Catholics (as opposed to trying to convert people who were not Catholics) was one of the strongest findings of the research.

2. being Catholic

Benedict XVI re-emphasised the need for charities to get the permission of the Church to use the term "Catholic" to describe their work. This does not stop other charities with a Catholic inspiration or origin continuing to make that claim without being answerable to the Church. In practice, even those charities who do still call themselves Catholic exhibit a significant range in how they envisage their Catholic ethos. How the Church relates to all these charities, including those who are not recognised as Catholic, given the symbiotic relationship between Church and charity, warrants further consideration.

There was a noticeable range in recognition of the importance of a Catholic ethos even within the same charities, with the concerns of trustees and strategic staff sometimes varying significantly from those of other staff and volunteers. Ethos became particularly difficult when it came to clashes on particular policies and doctrines. For example, the attitude of a charity on issues like divorce, homosexuality, abortion, working with other faiths and those of no faith, and how those attitudes come into conflict with either public opinion, local government policy or the views of service users was a tricky balance for a number of charities.

The other side of the issue was the actual relationship of charities with the Church. To a great extent there is a symbiotic relationship between charity and Church. At a local level the funding and volunteer base for Catholic charities remains heavily reliant on Church money or at least networks. In turn charities provide a public face of Catholic social action and serve a critical role as crucibles of evangelisation.

Relationships with the Church could prove to be immensely beneficial to charities, helping with promotion, public prominence, connections with other charities and being part of a broader movement. Where relations had broken down, however, charities could feel let down by the Church and denied those advantages that might have helped them to increase their impact. A new consideration of how the Church supports all Catholic charities and those charities inspired by Catholicism (even if they are no longer "Catholic" charities) especially in the light of the inevitable symbiotic relationship between Church and charity, is in order.

3. challenges facing Catholic charities

1. practical challenges

A reduction in available funding from local government as a result of cuts has had a significant impact on social action charities. The knock on effect of this has seen charities forced to work on an ever expanding range of issues previously under the remit of local government or other agencies, with a decreasing pool of available funders. More broadly Catholic charities are having to work harder than ever before to secure volunteers and funding not least because parish decline in many areas has reduced the available volunteer pool and funding base. The nature of funding is now that many charities require constant expansion and applications for new projects, which in the long-run may prove unsustainable.

There is as a result an urgent need for some charities to rethink volunteer recruitment and fundraising in the light of difficulties in maintaining congregations. Related to this is the difficulty in balancing volunteers and paid staff. Paid staff are expensive but have more time to offer for the work.

Catholic charities have a serious problem in raising public awareness outside the Church. This was recognised by the charities themselves, but was an ongoing problem as they sought to be better known in non-Catholic circles.

2. religious challenges

Senior Catholic charity staff saw a need for development in the Church in empowering and resourcing lay leadership.

There was also a sense in a number of charities that Catholics had more work to do in finding good ways of working with non-Catholic faith groups.

Several charities continued to report secular tensions, in which their status as a faith charity was negatively perceived. The evidence was, however, mixed, with some interviewees detecting a notable improvement in recent years, perhaps tied to austerity and the need for local government to find any partner that could help.

3. intellectual challenges

The spectre of the Catholic sex abuse scandal continues to have a significant negative impact on Catholic charities. Dealing with that historical issue, and other general perceptions of what "Catholicism" means was a real challenge in reaching some people.

There has been a move across the charity sector towards greater professionalism. This comes with its own challenges. On the one hand charities want to prove the competence and skill of their staff and volunteers to deal with difficult issues. On the other there is a concern to avoid becoming too clinical and professional at the expense of the personal relationships that make Catholic charities what they are.

recommendations

- The place of Catholic charities and their ethos and identity is one of growing importance. For the Church Catholic charities are increasingly serving as the primary locus of Christian involvement in public life. Given the declining sizes of congregations (at least outside London), the shortage of priests and the struggles of the religious orders and pressures on faith schools, Catholic charities increasingly are becoming the public representatives of the Church. This heightens the need for further clarification on the issue of what it means to have a Catholic ethos and how the Church resources and supports its charities.

- This will take on a particular relevance on those potential clash issues, particularly on issues of sexuality, conceptions of marriage, contraception and working with organisations of other faiths and of no faith. Finding a balance that allows charities to retain their Catholicity and still be able to operate with others who do not share

- (or are even actively opposed to) those commitments should be a key priority of the Church, charities and secular bodies.

- Catholic charities serve as crucibles of evangelisation – providing a space in which Catholic spirituality is grown and expressed. Charities do not necessarily do much to evangelise non-Catholics, but certainly have a profound impact on growing the faith within Catholic staff and volunteers. Given this, there is scope for an increasing appreciation of what the Church already has in its charities. In the cause of deepening Catholic spirituality and engaging younger Catholics the role of charities deserves greater consideration.

- The evidence on how charities embody CST should give cause for optimism, and offer space for significantly more interaction. Certainly there is evidence of Catholic charities genuinely embodying the principles of the option for the poor, solidarity, subsidiarity, personalism, family and evangelisation in innovative and powerful ways. There is also, however, a gap between some of the depth of content behind those ideas in CST and how they are actually understood in practice which could usefully be bridged by the Church, perhaps in the production of a new resource or pamphlet that looks at what CST means in the specific context of the Catholic charitable sector.

- There is a visibility and resource issue for Catholic charities. The evidence suggests significantly more work is needed in raising the profile of Catholic charities beyond only a Catholic audience. This is particularly urgent when parish decline in some areas is likely to have a serious impact on the volunteer and funding base available to Catholic charities.

Between the Church and Catholic charities is a symbiotic relationship which has challenges, both in terms of realising the principles of Catholic Social Teaching and in a host of other practical, religious and intellectual challenges not all of which are unique to Catholic charities. It is also one of enormous opportunity and potential – for the Church to see the way CST can be used and the Catholic faith embedded in society, and for charities to gain the intellectual and spiritual (as well as practical) support of the Church to fulfil their work.

executive summary – references

1 See the *Motu Proprio* by Benedict XVI "On the Service of Charity" issued 2012.

introduction

why this project?

Catholic Social Teaching (CST) has been having a period in the public intellectual limelight. Certainly political economics is now an area in which there are a number of voices advocating CST values as a solution to some of the current economic crises.[1] This perhaps reached a high point at a conference on 'Inclusive Capitalism' in 2014, co-hosted by the City of London Corporation and EL Rothschild investment firm. That conference included such speakers as the Governor of the Bank of England, Mark Carney, and the Head of the IMF, Christine Lagarde, both of whom spoke approvingly of the lessons of CST for the world market.

Carney spoke about the need for trust and responsibility in the market,[2] while Lagarde has quoted Pope Francis's critiques of excesses in capitalism on a number of occasions.[3] Carney and Lagarde are practicing Catholics, yet there are also more surprising advocates, and ones from a remarkably broad political spectrum. Non-Catholic Labour leaders including Lord Maurice Glasman[4] and the political economist and New Labour thinker Will Hutton[5] stand alongside more conservative non-Catholic voices like Phillip Blond[6] in advocating particular aspects of CST. All this interest has been aided and abetted by the strident and powerful criticisms of capitalism by Pope Francis since becoming Pope, and his undeniable popularity.

This is not the first time CST has come to have a powerful voice in the political debate. The European project of the 1950s, with its explicit appeal to solidarity and subsidiary (the latter term drawn explicitly from a Papal encyclical[7]) owed much to CST, as did the development of the welfare state in many Catholic West European nations after World War Two.[8]

However, it is a mistake to view CST as a tool only for political economists and theorists. This is not simply a package of ideas to be applied in a top down way by politicians. Social teaching is precisely that, teaching that pertains to social interaction – to the question of how we live together and relate to one another. This is an issue for all levels of society and for individuals, perhaps particularly individual Christians who are explicitly called to love their neighbour as themselves and for whom the concept of "the poor" is not simply a technical calculation but the group most particularly of concern to Jesus.

It is with that in mind that this project set out to look at Catholic charities. Catholic charities represent a critical part of Catholic engagement in the world around them. They are also by their very nature practical operations, seeking to change something concrete. For a study in how CST is embodied they represent, as a result, a fascinating example since they demonstrate both a deliberate Catholic ethos and active engagement in "real world" activity (as opposed to economic or political theory).

Most fundamentally they give a physical manifestation of Christianity. In this they echo the words of Benedict XVI in *Deus caritas est* who declared that "Being Christian is not the result of an ethical choice or lofty idea, but the encounter with an event, a person, which gives life a new horizon and decisive direction."[9] They are in a sense the manifestation and the echo of God's own love for his creation.

In looking to Catholic charities we hoped to see evidence of how CST principles were embedded in practice (whether consciously or unconsciously) and so to learn which principles worked well, which were more difficult to accomplish and where, if anywhere, Catholic charities' experience on the ground might provide lessons to the Church (and to academia) on how the theories might be built upon.

The intention was also to expand further, however, beyond simply looking at CST to broader questions of what it means to be a Catholic charity in Britain today (chapter 2) and what challenges and obstacles such charities face that limit their ability to do more (chapter 3).

The overall picture that emerges is of the enormous resource that the Church has in its charities – as tools to embody in practice the intellectual capital of CST that is often left to academic and Church debates as if their real world application was somehow a secondary concern. This resource is a powerful one, but one that faces a myriad of pressures and concerns, some as a result of secular and policy pressures, some more tied up in Catholicism itself. There is a need for the Church to assess what it has and how it interacts with its charities as well as for charities to continue to reflect on CST and their own Catholic identity.

Catholic social teaching

In one sense there is no such thing as Catholic Social Teaching. Or more accurately, since all theology and all Church teaching is concerned with God, God's creation and how humanity ought to act in relation to that, all theology has social implications. Catholic teaching has never, therefore, in any real sense *not* been social. That recognised, some parts of doctrine are more 'social' than others, in that they are particularly concerned with "transforming social realities with the power of the Gospel".[10]

What has come to be called Catholic Social Teaching (CST) are, therefore, those aspects of teaching that particularly concern issues of wealth, equality, social justice, and social organisation. As a sub-genre of Church teaching, it is generally considered in its modern form, to have started with Pope Leo XIII's 1891 encyclical *Rerum novarum*. Since that famous encyclical that provided criticism of both socialism and capitalism and showed a particular concern for the rights and condition of workers, the canon has steadily increased with a succession of papal encyclicals on a range of themes, most recently culminating in Pope Francis's *Laudato si'* that focused on capitalism, social justice and care of "our common home".

What defines the particular teachings that together make up CST is a matter of debate, but for the purpose of our research we set out with five primary themes to explore:

1. The Option for the Poor
2. Solidarity
3. Subsidiarity
4. Personalism
5. Family

Over the course of the research, and in response to what we were finding in the interviews, a sixth theme was added:

6. Evangelisation

Each of these themes will be defined and discussed in more detail in chapter 1 below.

Catholic charities

The Catholic charitable sector in the UK is enormous. Among the many sorts of Catholic charity that exist are the Dioceses, the various religious orders (Jesuits, Dominicans, etc.), a number of Catholic schools, social action charities (with a range as broad as social action itself), chaplaincies, higher education colleges and universities (including Heythrop College, London and St Mary's University Twickenham), scouts, campaign groups, chapels, family and marriage organisations, and many others. Searching by the word "Catholic" on the Charity Commission website brings up 388 hits, but excludes many that have a soft Catholic ethos or origin that doesn't appear under the specific wording on the commission website. It also, of course, excludes many aspects of charitable social action work which are not formally registered charities. For example, the innumerable acts of service by individual Catholics done in care and service for family, the elderly and neighbours.

Providing a study that took in that full range would be an impossible task. In order to get into some depth on these themes, we partnered with six Catholic charities. Given the sheer scale of Catholic charity work it is not possible to claim that these are a fully representative sample of all Catholic social action in Britain. However, they do represent a range of areas of interest, sizes and conceptions of their own Catholicity.

In total we conducted more than 70 interviews across the charities as well as observing several different activities and visiting various sites at which they were operating. With each charity we sought a range of interviewees. For larger charities this range included strategic level interviewees (trustees, senior management etc.), staff and volunteers and service users. For smaller charities in practice often the distinction between the strategic level and staff and volunteers was not a meaningful one, and the two marriage charities were both staffed by volunteers who had themselves also been (and continued to be) service users.

The six charities were:

- **Apostleship of the Sea (AoS).** The Apostleship of the Sea works supporting seafarers in Britain's ports. It provides chaplaincy and ship visiting services to all of Britain's ports. It is an agency of the Catholic Bishops' Conferences of England and Wales and Scotland, within which it is linked to the Department of International Affairs. It was founded in 1922.

- **Caritas Archdiocese of Birmingham.** Caritas Birmingham is the youngest of our charities, having been started as a network for Catholic social action work in the Birmingham Archdiocese by Archbishop Longley in October 2014. It is also the smallest of our charities, and the only one that is not a registered charity.

- **Father Hudson's Care (FHC).** Father Hudson's functions as the social care agency for the Archdiocese of Birmingham. It is closely connected to Caritas Birmingham, for which it functions as the secretariat. FHC is a long-established charity with deep roots in the Birmingham area, having originally started in 1902 specifically to look after homeless Catholic children. Today it works in a wide range of social care work, including with adults with disabilities, schools, children, young people and families, fostering, the elderly and a range of community-based projects.

- **Retrouvaille England and Wales.** Retrouvaille is a marriage crisis charity that works to help couples with serious marital difficulties. It was founded in Canada in the 1970s. Retrouvaille works closely with marriage and family life officers in dioceses but is not listed as a Catholic charity on the Charity Commission website.

- **The Saint Vincent de Paul Society (SVP).** The SVP is one of Britain's (and the world's) largest and best known Catholic charities. It has around 8,000 members who work on a range of social action work, but is best known for visiting individuals and families. In 2013-14 that amounted to supporting 81,308 individuals and families across 579,664 hours of voluntary service.[11] It is also the oldest of our charities, having operated in England and Wales since 1844 and internationally since 1833.

- **Worldwide Marriage Encounter (WWME).** Like Retrouvaille, WWME is a marriage charity whose primary focus is on enriching and refreshing the relationships of couples who are engaged, married, or in long-standing relationships. It also works with couples preparing for marriage. The website and charity commission page are more explicitly Catholic than Retrouvaille and it has been registered as a charity in the UK since 1976.

For our study that provides a significant range in size, from the very small (Retrouvaille had an income for 2015 listed on the Charity Commission website of just over £24,000) to the very large (the SVP's income for 2015 was £9.5 million). It also gives a good scope of activity, from marriage and family support through to chaplaincy work (the AoS) and more traditional social action work confronting issues such as poverty (SVP), disability (FHC) and others. Finally it gives a range in terms of links with the Church. The AoS sits as a part of the Catholic Bishops' Conference, while WWME is not a member even of networks like CSAN (Caritas Social Action Network – a body serving as a network for Catholic social action work in the UK). The SVP is in CSAN and is well-known as a Catholic charity, but unlike FHC or the AoS has no official Church representative among its trustees.

Finally this range of charities gives a difference in terms of interaction with government and secular bodies. Caritas Birmingham is not even a registered charity, and the two marriage charities have fairly minimal interaction with public bodies. By contrast FHC has a significant relationship with local government in regards to a number of its care services, including its work on disability, in schools and with the elderly.

This first, and longest, section of this report looks at the embedding of CST principles in practice in the six charities. It looks at the extent to which CST principles are identifiable and consciously embodied in charitable work. It considers in turn six themes of CST: The option for the poor, solidarity, subsidiarity, personalism, family and evangelisation. Each of those functions as a meta-theme containing a number of subsidiary themes. This section constitutes by far the largest part of the report, since it was on those questions of CST and how far the principles of CST were realised that the research was primarily focused.

The second section looks at the question of how the charities themselves view their broader Catholic ethos and relationships with the Church. Essentially it asks the question what does it mean to call yourself a "Catholic charity"? Again, the evidence for this is drawn primarily from interviews with practitioners from the six partner charities, though the official stance of the Church as seen in documents like *Deus caritas est* and *Caritas in veritate* is also considered.

The final section looks at the challenges facing the six charities, both practical and more theoretical, that prevent them from working as effectively as they otherwise might. It is divided into three themes; one of which looks at practical barriers to the effectiveness of charities, including funding problems and issues related to austerity politics. The second theme covers religious challenges, that is those challenges that particularly affect these charities on account of being FBOs (Faith-Based Organisations). Finally, the section on intellectual challenges covers those issues that do not necessarily require an immediate response but function in the background as things that concern or limit charities.

introduction – references

1. See for example Clifford Longley, *Just Money: How Catholic Social Teaching can Redeem Capitalism* (Theos, 2014).
2. Inclusive capitalism address 2014.
3. At the same conference, for example, she quoted Pope Francis's phrase that inequality was the "root of social evil".
4. Among a number of examples see his paper 'Catholic Social Thought as Political Economy' delivered at Durham University in May 2013 and available online: https://www.dur.ac.uk/resources/theology.religion/LordGlasmansLectureonCatholicSocialTeachingasPolitical Economy.pdf (accessed 10/12/2015).
5. Will Hutton, *How good we can be: Ending the Mercenary Society and Building a Great Country* (Little Brown) 2015.
6. Phillip Blond, *Red Tory: How Left and Right have Broken Britain and How we can Fix It* (Faber & Faber, 2010).
7. The term was suggested as a building block of a European project by French politician Pierre-Henri Teitgen in 1953
8. Kees van Kersbergen and Philip Manow, *Religion, Class Coalitions, and Welfare States* (Cambridge University Press, 2009).
9. Benedict XVI, *Deus caritas est (2005)* 1.
10. From the Presentation of *The Compendium of the Social Doctrine of the Church* produced by the Pontifical Council for Justice and Peace (2004) p. xvii.
11. Data from SVP Trustees' Report 2014.

CST in practice

As laid out in the introduction, we explored six themes of Catholic Social Teaching across our six charities. What follows is an outline of each of those themes, explaining how they were understood in our research, the extent to which they were embodied in different charitable settings, and areas in which the experience of charities at the coalface of British public life might broaden the academic and Church debates on these issues.

1. the option for the poor

The Option for the Poor is the idea that God and the Church have a particular concern and duty for the poor. *Rerum novarum* defines part of the duty of the Church as having a particular need to support the poor:

> When there is a question of protecting the rights of individuals, the poor and helpless have a claim to special consideration. The rich population has many ways of protecting themselves, and stands less in need of help.[1]

This message is consistently echoed throughout CST, and Pope Francis's *Evangelii gaudium* continues the theme when it proclaims:

> the Church has made an option for the poor which is understood as a 'special form of primacy in the exercise of Christian charity, to which the whole tradition of the Church bears witness.'[2]

This commitment to the poor seems like an obvious starting point for charities, particularly those that are social action charities, and indeed the SVP is among those charities with an explicit commitment to challenging poverty. Its charitable object as listed on the Charity Commission is "the relief of poverty, both material and emotional".[3]

That charitable objective itself raises an interesting issue, however, which is how "the poor" is to be understood. Catholic theology has a long history of exploring question of what it is to be poor and to take the option for the poor, with liberation theology being a particularly well known exploration of that question. Throughout our interviews we discovered a consistently nuanced approach to the issue of the poor and marginalised. Alongside the obvious idea of poverty as material and financial need, which was addressed in several charities, four additional themes in particular emerged:

1. Relational poverty/poverty of isolation
2. Poverty as being on the margins
3. Spiritual poverty
4. The ubiquity of poverty

> Throughout our interviews we discovered a consistently nuanced approach to the issue of the poor and marginalised.

Not all of these were present in all of the charities, or among all of the interviewees. Some charities have a particular vision that leads them to focus particularly on some aspects more than others. The nature of the charity's service users will obviously define a lot of the way the charity thinks about poverty. Hence Caritas Birmingham, which doesn't directly have any service users but instead functions as a network to connect and support local social action charities, does less direct work on poverty and what it means to be poor (though they have led on projects empowering other organizations to work on homelessness) than a charity like the SVP, which is explicitly focused on alleviating types of poverty, or the Apostleship of the Sea, which has a very clear set of service users in seafarers at Britain's ports.

1. relational poverty/poverty of isolation

Countering isolation and a poverty of relationships is central to the work of the SVP. Much of their work involves members visiting those who are vulnerable and lonely and befriending them over a sustained period of time. In contrast to other services, and particularly government agencies, one of the SVP's great advantages is the ability to commit significant time and effort to sitting with and getting to know their service users. Whereas other services might only be available during periods of particular crisis, the SVP makes a point of consistently visiting people, regardless of how urgent any particular meeting might be.

The causes of isolation and vulnerability can vary significantly. The SVP is divided at the local level into conferences that generally sit within a particular Catholic parish. As a result the sort of issue they respond to can vary significantly depending on local need. Many do much of their work visiting and supporting the elderly within their local area. However, there is recognition that the sources of isolation are broad and include, among others, material poverty (in so far as it prevents full participation in local life), age, disability, dementia, illness and health problems, language barriers, or having recently arrived as a refugee or immigrant. Different SVP groups were involved in all of those issues.

One volunteer shared the example of a woman who sought help from their SVP group. She was suffering with depression and anxiety but for various reasons had been unable to secure any government help. She was a lapsed Catholic (which was how she had heard of the SVP), and had no friends or family in the local area. As a result she was entirely isolated which only added to her problems. The SVP visits "virtually turned her life around in nine months!" Most of what they did was simply listening, but they also found ways to include her in local activities and helped decorate her flat for her. Now she no longer "lives behind closed doors" in the words of the volunteer.

The SVP's focus is very explicit in countering isolation and loneliness, but this idea of relational poverty was present in other charities too. Father Hudson's Care covers a range of services but has increasingly been working to support community projects throughout the diocese. One of these is part of a wider project based in a parish centre in Clayton and consists of little more than a phone used to contact elderly residents in the area and stay in touch with them. It's a small project, which costs little, but makes a huge difference to those people who are called – it challenges the isolation that can blight people's lives.

The Apostleship of the Sea provides pastoral care to seafarers in British ports. Much of this is very practical, like providing SIM cards and internet access so that seafarers can call home, helping with advice on things like currency transactions and identifying the right people to help in labour disputes. However, one of the most critical aspects of the work is simply being there for those whose lives are defined by transience. Ships do not tend, in today's highly mechanised world, to need to stay in port for long. Some might only dock for a few hours. This is a hard and transient life, spent away from home or much meaningful contact with anyone other than shipmates, for months at a time. In such a context, the ability of chaplains to provide friendship and presence is a critical tool in countering this relational poverty.

> *Poverty was never envisaged in purely material terms and the danger of isolation and prevalence of relational poverty was of significant concern to several of them.*

This was a significant theme in how charities viewed their obligation to the poor and the option for the poor. Poverty was never envisaged in purely material terms and the danger of isolation and prevalence of relational poverty was of significant concern to several of them.

2. poverty as being on the margins

Closely tied to the idea of relational poverty is a sense of the Christian duty to go to the margins. The poor are not necessarily materially poor so much as the most marginalised figures in society.

Some of the causes of this marginality are very similar to those that define isolation – our charities worked, for example, with a range of clients that included the disabled, refugees and asylum seekers, drug and alcohol addicts and a range of others including many who in the words of one charity trustee are "perhaps the hard people to love" or those who another interviewee described as "those that society tells you they don't want – like the asylum seekers".

Several of the charities were very conscious indeed of this special calling to the margins. The Apostleship of the Sea, for example, at a conference for its chaplains had a reflection on the lessons of Luke's gospel, in which Christ appears first to those most on the margins – widows, women, children, outsiders and lepers. Seafarers, one chaplain noted, operate in an "invisible world", one that is never seen by most British people, who rely on goods coming by sea but never think of the people bringing them.

Working conditions and rights upon cargo ships are desperately poor in the seafaring world. Seafarers become a very real expression of the margins, and for one chaplain a multiply marginal world – one that is both marginal in the sense of being on the edge of society but also on the edge of life and death. This is a dangerous industry in which death and injury are commonplace. Several chaplains shared stories of being called to ships after disasters. In one case, a sailor had investigated why the anchor was not working properly in a chamber in the ship and did not return. Another went to check and also did not return. Both, it transpired had suffocated – the chamber was full of rust that had absorbed all the air. In another case a sailor was crushed to death by a load of coal as it slipped when being unloaded.

If these examples are extreme they are nonetheless illustrative of a conscious call to the margins that was echoed in other charities. For one senior staff member at Father Hudson's this was expressed simply as "that's what comes of a Catholic charity – an explicit focus to find those who fall through the gaps and are on the margins". Father Hudson's Care in fact had some interesting examples of this, both in its homes, day centre and support work for adults with disabilities and in some of its community projects that worked closely with asylum seekers and immigrant groups. One such project, which in April 2015 become a charity in its own right having been supported by Father Hudson's (in partnership with the Sisters of Our Lady of Charity) for some years, is Anawim. Father Hudson's continue to provide support in some areas, and the Father Hudson's CEO is the Anawim Chair of Trustees at the current time.

Anawim (a name which itself is illustrative of the point, since it is an Aramaic word for the poor and the outcast) is a charity that works to support women in the criminal justice system, either in prison or in hostels or on the streets. It is a powerful example of the commitment of Catholic charities to the marginalised.

There is nothing especially novel in viewing the poor in terms of marginalisation, yet the witness of Catholic charity work on the ground does offer a vision of what that commitment means in practice. It is also notable that this talk of poverty as marginalisation was present, unprompted, in many interviews. The sense of "the poor" and the wider understanding of what that meant was at least one CST idea that had genuinely permeated throughout the organisations.

3. spiritual poverty

In 1984, the then Cardinal Joseph Ratzinger (later Pope Benedict XVI), in his role as prefect of the Congregation for the Doctrine of the Faith wrote his official response to the development of liberation theology in Latin America.[4] In it he criticised liberation theology for its failure to recognise that the ultimate liberation can never be earthly or material but must instead be from "the radical slavery of sin". For Ratzinger this failure to take seriously the spiritual element of all existence and poverty was a fundamental (and un-Catholic) error on the part of some liberation theologians.

This is a criticism that is worth taking seriously in relation to Catholic charity work. In chapter 2 below, there is a greater consideration of what it means to have a Catholic ethos and actually be a *Catholic* charity as opposed to any other sort of charity. It can be a point of very real tension in thinking about public perceptions of a charity and answering accusations of "proselytism" if there is a significant focus on spiritual and religious work alongside meeting material needs.[5]

That said, a sense of meeting spiritual poverty was present in quite a pronounced way in several of our charities. In the case of the AoS the importance of providing the explicitly religious service of the Catholic sacraments was one very highly valued by many of their service users. Filipino seafarers make up a significant portion of all seafarers coming through Britain's ports, and it is perhaps little surprise given how devoutly Catholic that country is that there is, in the words of one chaplain "a very real and humbling hunger for the sacraments". At the SVP several interviewees noted how much older clients in particular often explicitly asked for a more Catholic focus in their visits, perhaps asking for prayers, or singing hymns that they remembered from their youth.

For others there was a softer focus on spiritual needs, but one that remained embedded in their work. Interviewees from the SVP, Father Hudson's, and several of Father Hudson's community projects spoke about providing a holistic service and holistic care that looked at material *and* spiritual needs. One of Father Hudson's senior staff spoke about a desire throughout the organisation to care for the "whole person, that's not just their physical needs, or their psychological needs, but their spiritual ones too".

Perhaps the most interesting expression of this focus, however, came from the two marriage charities. Both Retrouvaille and Worldwide Marriage Encounter work with couples who for whatever reason are experiencing difficulties in their relationships. They take couples on retreats and lead them through a number of sessions presented by couples who have been through the same programme. The exercises are designed to find ways reconnect couples and help them communicate. The observation of one interviewee was that often the hardest part of the process was getting over one's own shame at doing something that had hurt a partner, rather than forgiving a partner for something they had done. The scheme works on loving oneself, loving each other, and sharing that love, but it is the first of those that proves the most difficult. This concern for self-forgiveness is self-evidently not a material concern; it lies within the realm of spiritual poverty.

It is notable that this aspect of poverty was one that was not universally recognised, with some staff and volunteers not mentioning any such aspect. However, it was certainly present among a large number of volunteers and strategic level interviewees at a number of charities. It is worth noting (as below in chapter 2) that the extent to which a Catholic ethos permeated through the charities did vary at different levels (i.e. some staff members were less attuned to the Catholic aspect than strategic level interviewees had been).

4. the ubiquity of poverty

In a sense this is more of a meta-theme, in that it is not itself a type of poverty as much as a guiding consideration of how to approach society. Essentially it is the idea that the poor are in a real sense everywhere, not simply some theoretical group of people. It is perhaps best summarised by a trustee of the SVP who said:

> Our greatest challenge is priests who say 'I don't need an SVP group; there are no poor in my parish'. We find this ignorant and upsetting. Bereavement, ill-health, isolation, this is irrespective of wealth – they are *poor*.

There was a sense in a number of our charities of the poor being everywhere, even in unexpected places. At Father Hudson's Care one of their community projects is the charity Brushstrokes that works in Smethwick. That project is designed to seek out the "hidden poor," that is those people in need who are not obvious, because their situation is happening behind closed doors and isn't widely known. One volunteer described this idea in some depth:

> I didn't know half of what was going on here. My sons are now thirty and went to school here, where I was a governor, just round the corner from Brushstrokes, and yet, I had no idea of some of the conditions in which local people were living. The guest houses are full to bursting with asylum seekers; I didn't know that. [I] didn't know there was a local drugs problem. When they go to school or work they put their best face on – so we don't see it.

There is a sense here of something that we will return to in considering solidarity below, the idea that Christian responsibility and the option for the poor has to orient itself towards the extent to which this poverty is ubiquitous, present in all communities, even if it is not obvious.

Finally on this idea of ubiquity it is important to note that "the poor", however they are understood, cannot be seen as a group to be helped that is somehow distinct from the rest of society. Those who work or volunteer for charities are not somehow differentiated from the poor – there is no "us and them." This is often the criticism of charities that in practice they represent a patronising attitude towards a particular group in society.

2. solidarity

Solidarity is perhaps the most familiar term drawn from CST, sharing a similar conception in some ways to the socialist concept of the same name. Inherent within the Catholic idea is a particular conception of the "common good" and of compassion (not simply sympathy but literal com-passion – an idea of suffering alongside). In the 1987 encyclical *Sollicitudo rei socialis* by John Paul II this concept was described with the statement:

> We are all one family in the world. Building a community that empowers everyone to attain their full potential through each of us respecting each other's dignity, rights and responsibilities makes the world a better place to live.[6]

In a sense charities are an obvious place to look for solidarity; they after all represent action taken to help others, which is solidarity by definition. Again, though, what is interesting about the way in which our interviewees discussed this idea was how it broke down into a number of further themes that provide a more nuanced understanding of what solidarity means in practice. These were:

1. The "Common Good"

2. Neighbourliness

3. Solidarity in practice (practical and spiritual aid)

4. Advocacy and being the voice of the voiceless.

The terminology in question was not always as it appeared in interviews, though some terms, notably "solidarity" and "common good" certainly came up with regularity, even if the content behind the terminology was sometimes a bit thin.

1. the "Common Good"

Perhaps no single piece of CST terminology has been as (over)used as the idea of the "common good". It essentially denotes the idea of building a just and fair society that operates for the benefit of everyone.[7] More specifically it holds that the fulfilment of humanity is fundamentally found "in common" with others – that is to say that a good society cannot be reduced to the benefits obtained for any one individual. The good for an individual is only attainable through the exercise of common effort with others (see also the related ideas in personalism below). So, for example, the *Compendium of the Social Doctrine of the Church* calls for the state to have a role in society since "the individual person, the family, or intermediate groups are not able to achieve their full development by themselves for living a truly human life".[8]

Naturally, how to understand that in practice becomes difficult. No doubt that explains in part how the term has come to find itself so frequently employed across the political spectrum in quite different contexts.

Nevertheless, the common good is still an idea with motivating power, and there was certainly in our interviews a conception of Catholic charity as working for the common good – as a contribution towards creating a better society, more fully embodying the values of the Gospel. A senior staff member at the Apostleship of the Sea noted how the senior staff and trustees of that charity meet regularly to think through those issues explicitly in the light of CST. They had reflected on Pope Francis's *Evangelii gaudium* and were also preparing at the time of interview to reflect on *Laudato si'*.

As an idea it was certainly a motivation behind Caritas Birmingham. Caritas was set up in the Birmingham Archdiocese by Archbishop Longley in 2014 as a response to the 2012 call of Pope Benedict XVI to set up more Caritas networks to enable and support Catholic charitable activity.[9] It functions as a network for Catholic charitable activity across the Diocese, providing advice and resources and services like twinning projects working on similar themes. The overall motivation was described by one of its board as quite simply representing the responsibility of Catholics to get involved in creating the common good since "we have responsibility. You can't just pay your taxes and wash your hands".

The Brushstrokes community project at Father Hudson's took its name out of a similar motivation. The idea is that each contribution towards making society a better place, no matter how small, is another brushstroke that adds to the overall canvas, even if the whole picture is only truly visible to the artist (God).

Broadly speaking interviewees, other than a few at a strategic level, did not have a particularly deep or nuanced understanding of the term "common good".

The work of the SVP and Father Hudson's community projects are good examples of direct involvement in building a society for the common good. The SVP's shops are a particularly interesting example. These stores, of which the SVP now has over 40, including 11 in the Leeds Diocese employ around 100 people and also provide work experience and volunteering opportunities for others so that they can get references for other jobs. That in itself is a useful service, but they also sell second-hand furniture for people in more deprived areas to buy at low prices, while raising awareness of the charity.

Broadly speaking interviewees, other than a few at a strategic level, did not have a particularly deep or nuanced understanding of the term "common good" – though its use was common. For many what it implied was obvious, and not worth prolonged consideration – it simply meant working to improve society and communities in the broadest possible sense. This raises the possibility of more work being done to crystallise a Catholic understanding of the common good as it relates to charitable work.

2.   neighbourliness

If the common good represents the idea of working for a fairer and more just society, neighbourliness in the sense it is used here denotes the underlying attitude that makes that commitment possible.[10] A critical element in this is love. A senior member of staff at the AoS described their work as "going to where people really *are*... and taking a cargo of love". This was echoed by interviewees from WWME who described their work as being a "freely given gift of love from the Church to society".

Part of this is expressed in other ways, for example simply by virtue of availability. Though all of our charities identified themselves as Catholic charities, all were keen to insist that they would work for everyone. Indeed for several of them, that was an official rule. For the two marriage charities an essential aspect of their work lay in a non-judgemental attitude that would accept any of the couples regardless of their history. For some this availability was as simple as being the only available service. Seafarers have access to very little pastoral and practical support save that provided by port chaplains and ship visitors such as those provided by the AoS. In another example, one interviewee mentioned that on the estate in which the Hope project (one of the Father Hudson's community projects) was based it represented the only open door that people could go to. For an SVP interviewee, similarly, the importance of the charity was in its ability to "get behind the closed doors".

A final aspect of this necessary attitude of neighbourliness is a sense of self-responsibility. Partly this sense of responsibility is, as already discussed, to get involved at all and take action for the common good. More than that, however, one aspect of solidarity is the sense of taking responsibility for one's own history. In the case of Father Hudson's Care this is a relevant concern because that charity has changed significantly over time. In its earlier years as a charity that ran a home for homeless Catholic children it exhibited a model of care that was of its era, but is not one that would exist today. The charity has not run any such homes since the 1980s, but there is an ongoing legacy from those homes that cannot be ignored, in particular a sex abuse scandal that saw a priest jailed in 1998 for various offences committed within the home against young boys.

In our interviews there was no effort to deny or defend those past events, but rather one trustee said that the service they were most pleased with from their time at Father Hudson's was the establishment of the Origins service. This service provides support for all people who were once either residents in the homes or went through the charity's adoption services. Despite no longer providing either the homes or an adoption service it demonstrates an ongoing concern for the charity's responsibility to those children who were once in its care.

3. solidarity in practice (practical and spiritual aid)

In talking about solidarity one theme of many interviews was the need to temper it with a sense of realism. There is a danger in all charity work that a desire to help can outstrip prudence and a real appreciation of what is possible. A trustee at Father Hudson's Care was very clear on this danger, in which a lot of people are very enthusiastic and eager and have ideas that are motivated by solidarity, but sometimes need to be pulled back a little for the sake of a long-term vision of solidarity. The alternative is to run out of money and ultimately let down many people already reliant on the charity.

This is true also of the necessary flexibility in what sort of work is done. Solidarity needs to take seriously what sort of action is most necessary, not simply what the charity has always done. Several charities demonstrated that in practice. Father Hudson's changed its model of care from something that was, in the words of some interviewees, a "paternalist" model to something more modern and concerned with people being involved in choosing their own care. The SVP in many of its local conferences had recognised that solidarity meant changing the service users it worked with depending on local need. Many were now doing far more work with asylum seekers than they had previously.

Flexibility is also a theme at the Apostleship of the Sea. The intention is to be relational and provide quality pastoral care to seafarers, but how to deliver that in practice has had to be flexible. In order to be able to reach people and help as effectively as possible the service has had to evolve according to need. At present, one aspect of that is providing very practical assistance with means of communication home. Previously that involved help at the seafarers' centre, today it is more likely to involve providing internet access on the ship, or SIM cards and internet cards for use with phones that the seafarers already own. Even that, however, it was widely suspected was a model that was probably on the way out, with more and more ships now able to provide their own Wi-Fi.

4. advocacy and being the voice of the voiceless

One final aspect of solidarity worth discussing is the dimension of moving beyond providing a service, to advocating on behalf of a group or cause. In each of our six charities this was a secondary consideration that ranked below other aspects of their work. However, there was in several an increasing sense that this was an oversight, and that actually speaking up to change the situation was an important aspect of their work. At its most basic, the logic is that if by advocacy you can cause a change that will prevent a problem from existing then it is clearly a good thing to do so, a basic version of prevention rather than cure. There is also a second basic element of solidarity to this, which is that the people with whom these charities are working, by virtue of their position on the margins of society, are often those least able to speak up for themselves and, therefore, need someone else to do it on their behalf.

It might also be helpful on advocacy to think in terms of justice. In this it should be noted that Catholic teaching, particularly in Benedict XVI's *Deus caritas est,* draws a distinction between the work of justice and charity.[11] Justice, the formation of a just society, is the domain of politics, while charity remains in the domain of the Church. The direct intervention of the Church is limited to the latter, with the political domain being left to the lay faithful. This distinction is a difficult one in practice. Charities, for one thing, are also increasingly the domain of the lay faithful. What exactly constitutes direct intervention is also a difficult balance to draw. Our case studies were not political actors, but there was a real sense in which part of their *caritas* work demanded a greater focus on advocacy and being a voice for the voiceless. Justice and charity are, in practice, mutually necessary in the work of Catholic charities.

At the SVP this was certainly an area of concern raised by several interviewees. It is an explicit role of the charity to be "a voice for the voiceless" (an expression that arose frequently in interviews both at the SVP and elsewhere), and yet in interviews at all levels of the organisation it was felt that this was an area that needed more work. This was already being addressed at the strategic level. The elephant in the room for the SVP and Father Hudson's was the effect of austerity policies on particular segments of society. This raised a particular challenge in speaking out without being seen as a political campaigning organisation.

In both cases they had been more successful in being advocates in a more private way, by fighting battles with local government and other bodies on behalf of their service users. An observation of a number of staff and volunteers at both charities was that the forms and procedures for claiming benefits and other services had become extremely difficult and there was a lack of help for vulnerable people trying to apply. Both had done significant amounts of work supporting people to fill in documents and in some cases actively appealing to local government.

One story from a staff member at Father Hudson's illustrated that issue particularly well:

> One example: we had a severely disabled man who was using the day centre and one day he got a letter from the council saying they were stopping his funding to come to the day service. [There was] no real explanation, no consultation, no replacement provision – they just stopped. And that really distressed his mother as well. Well we appealed on his behalf, but while we were appealing we let him keep using the services for nothing – because we could and it was the right thing to do. His mother is in her 70s. How can she take on Birmingham council? It would have very difficult and very distressing for her.

This challenge of having some success in private advocacy but more difficulty in getting across a public message was also replicated at the Apostleship of the Sea. Working conditions for seafarers are poor, and that is something the AoS are keen to advocate about, but in practice it has been difficult to get the word out, particularly outside of a Catholic audience. There are campaigns, and "Sea Sunday" – an annual day at which churches remember, pray and raise money for seafarers, which is a critical event in both raising profile and funding the AoS activities.

AoS also have a good record of appearing in the Catholic press and the national office has a role in raising the overall profile. However, interviewees noted that there was more to be done to spread the word and highlight the work of seafarers and to confront the problem of what chaplains described as an "invisible world". Few British people work as seafarers, and even those who work in the ports in practice might have little contact with those who live and work on the ships. Their work is broadly invisible to the British public. Finding ways to get more public profile is a major challenge for this aspect of solidarity.

That challenge was seen at the two marriage charities as well. There, a lack of people and resources to raise profile was seen as a particular challenge in putting out their message about the importance of marriage and family life, and the service they provided in supporting both. There were exceptions: both charities had had some success in advertising on Christian radio, and mixed success in using diocesan structures to advertise in churches (warmth seemed to vary from diocese to diocese). Both also had their own advocates among marriage and family life officers at some dioceses and some bishops, but both had interviewees who lamented the lack of further support and saw that as a barrier to more work.

3. subsidiarity

The idea of subsidiarity comes from a number of encyclicals but is perhaps most clearly defined in Pius XI's 1932 document *Quadragesimo anno:*

> Just as it is gravely wrong to take from individuals what they can accomplish by their own initiative and industry and give it to the community, so also it is an injustice and at the same time a grave evil and disturbance of right order to assign to a greater and higher association what lesser and subordinate organizations can do.[12]

Subsidiarity functions for CST essentially as a corrective to twentieth century political discourses. Against socialism it puts forward the idea that real justice is found in letting people and organisations take action for themselves where they are able to, thereby valuing non-state and local agency over the state. Against some models of capitalism, it also suggests that there is a place for different levels in society to take action; people are not simply isolated and expected to stand only on their own two feet. This obviously has consequences for political, welfare and economic structures in how they produce levels that are responsive to individuals and communities while retaining the ability for more centralised action where appropriate.

In applying this idea to the charities we came across two main themes:

1. Real localism
2. Appropriate agency

The term "subsidiarity" itself arose in a limited number of interviews (far fewer than used the idea of "solidarity"). It is fair to say that the term was often little understood in and of itself. There were exceptions to this general rule. Trustees and other strategic level interviewees were far more likely both to use the term and also to have a more in-depth understanding of what was meant by it.

However, the idea of localism and of being responsive to different needs at different levels (the underpinning idea of subsidiarity) was an idea that did come up frequently and was significantly valued by interviewees throughout. Given that subsidiarity is the term used in CST and the official Church and academic discourse there is clearly something of a gap to be crossed here in understanding the terminology.

1. real localism

A critical aspect of subsidiarity is the idea that local issues are best understood and addressed at a local level. This was strongly exhibited in several of our charities. A key defining feature of Caritas Birmingham is that it is a network designed to empower and support local projects. Part of the first thing they did after being founded in 2014 was to work on a consultation and mapping exercise to understand what projects already existed, and where problems existed. Subsequently the work has involved supporting those projects and finding ways of 'twinning' projects working on similar issues. There is plenty of scope for this small scale work supporting local projects, not least since, in the words of one interviewee:

> A lot of it isn't very innovative. Usually many of the local problems are the same and the solutions are often obvious – food, clothing, shelter and friendship. Not every project has to be incredibly exciting to be what's needed.

The SVP structure lends itself very well to such a model of subsidiarity rooted in local concerns. The whole structure of the society rests on work being done in local, parish-level conferences that are able to pick the issues most prevalent in their area to focus on. The result is that two conferences might work with completely different types of service user. Some work primarily or even solely with elderly people in their area, others with refugees and asylum seekers, for example. Even special projects like the furniture stores, for which a separate funding stream exists, begin with ideas and proposals from the grass roots, rather than being imposed by the national office.

The support of Father Hudson's Care for community projects reflects a similar desire to respond to local needs at a local level, and there was a marked enthusiasm among strategic level interviewees and trustees to see more such community projects in the future.

This commitment to local response was also reflected in a more surprising way in the two marriage charities. Both Retrouvaille and WWME try to establish local support groups for couples who have been through the scheme. It is fair to say that some of these efforts at establishing local groups had been more successful than others, depending both on how many couples involved in the scheme a particular local area actually has in it, and the level of enthusiasm for continuing engagement. It does, however, at the very least show a commitment to the idea that local support makes for more durable success.

The Apostleship of the Sea might seem like the awkward exception to this rule; after all, they are serving people who are by definition not local. They are also fundraising from far beyond the ports that have any direct interaction with coastal trade. However, as one chaplain put it they represent "the global encounter of global industry in a localised place". In that sense there remains a sort of localism intrinsic in the model, in that there is a strong sense of acting out a global issue on a local level.

2. appropriate agency

At the other end of the subsidiarity spectrum from a commitment to localism is the advantage of having structures that allow for economies of scale and taking wider action than a local project could deliver on some issues. Once again this is particularly relevant for the way in which Caritas Birmingham functions. It works by being a network that connects different projects across the diocese, twinning those working on similar issues and providing advice, training and resources on matters that concern all of them (such as writing charitable objectives, making grant applications, complying with employment and HR regulations, fulfilling legal obligations etc.).

One recent scheme of work was looking at homelessness across the diocese and the different projects involved in confronting it. Caritas Birmingham does not directly provide any services, but instead its whole function is to empower and support other projects and services. As such it serves a valuable function in supporting charities with advice and resources that come from shared expertise and experience in the sector. This allows small projects that might consist of only a limited number of volunteers in a parish setting to benefit from some of the advantages that would usually require a larger organisation with dedicated HR and legal support.

Father Hudson's Care provides a similar role for its community projects (and indeed also functions at the present time as the secretariat for Caritas Birmingham). By providing core funding, HR support, pay roll support, legal support and communications and publicity support for various locally-based projects, they are able to reduce such costs to these projects and empower their staff and volunteers. This is only possible because Father

Hudson's has an existing established office with full time finance and HR staff who are able to manage what is going on in the projects as well as Father Hudson's own staff.

Charities with national offices and established infrastructures are undoubtedly able to do larger scale and more professional fundraising and management of staff and volunteers. The danger then is in becoming detached from local issues and the volunteer base. For Caritas Birmingham and Father Hudson's, working with local projects rather than seeking to do much of the work directly is a way of meeting that concern. At the SVP, the national office is able to co-ordinate accounts and manage matters like DBS checks.[13] Critically, however, the charity tries to keep the national office small and to be clear that the actual work is co-ordinated according to local need at the level of the local parish conferences.

This economy of scale issue can also serve as a barrier for some charities. Even at Father Hudson's it was notable that many of the individual services were quite small. The fostering service, for example, was significantly smaller than other potential service providers in the area. This provides some advantages – not least the ability to retain personal and close relationships with all the carers and families in a way that would not have been possible had the service been bigger. It also has its disadvantages, small size and a correspondingly small budget making it hard to compete with some of the bigger providers.

This issue of size also hurt the marriage charities. Both are small bespoke services, which provide some clear advantages in retaining close and intimate relations with the couples. It also puts a significant strain on those couples expected to co-ordinate the charities. With no staff, the onus for responding to requests, organising the programme, keeping track of (and increasing) volunteers, training volunteers and actually running the weekend retreats falls on one or two volunteer couples and priests.

It is worth noting, however, in regard to subsidiarity, that despite the two marriage charities being small operations in the UK, they both sit within a broader international network. The same is true of the Apostleship of the Sea, which worldwide operates in more than 250 ports, and the SVP, which exists in 150 countries and has an estimated membership of more than 800,000.[14] This international dimension is a notable feature of many Catholic charities, undeniably helped by the international presence of the Church itself. It also provides some particular advantages. For the AoS, for example, the international presence allows for sharing of information about particular ships, so that chaplains in different countries are aware of some problems even before the ship in question arrives in port. For the marriage charities one observation of interviewees at Worldwide Marriage Encounter was that the different experiences and trajectories of the charity in different countries provided useful information on future challenges.

So, for example, challenges to the charity to accept homosexual couples on weekends (a situation which has not yet arisen for the British branch), or to have volunteer couples who were either not Catholic or mixed (i.e. one Catholic spouse, and one non-Catholic) have already been seen in other branches and provide clues as to what responses may be necessary. At the very least they might flag issues to think about, even if there are no easy answers to be drawn from those experiences.

4. personalism

Personalism is the idea that all human beings are essentially relational. A "person" as opposed to an "individual" is a unit that only exists in relation to others. Individualism prizes the individual as an overly independent, atomic figure who exists without the need for others. Personalism, by contrast, sees the individual as fundamentally interconnected and reliant on others. This is an idea with a long heritage, particularly within Thomist theology. St Thomas Aquinas saw the Trinity (following the earlier theologian Boethius) as three distinct persons, where a person is "an individual substance of a rational nature" who, critically, is in essential relation to other persons.

In the twentieth century Catholic theologians and philosophers, most notably Emmanuel Mounier[15] and Jacques Maritain[16] began to apply this more directly to the political and social sphere. Since humans are made in the image of God it stands to reason that humans too are essentially relational beings. They are not merely atomised individuals who are capable of operating in a vacuum, but instead are intrinsically in a constant dynamic relationship with other humans and with God. This also implies a sense of equal and inherent dignity in all human beings. This concept of personalism has developed throughout Catholic thought and underpins theologies as different as the liberation theologian Leonardo Boff's vision of society and politics (*Trinity and Society*[17]), and Pope John Paul II's idea of personhood and economics.[18]

For John Paul II the person becomes a unit in society that cannot be considered as something to be used, but as a being to which the only possible response is love (in direct contrast to Marxist and Utilitarian notions of the person as an economic unit operating towards a goal). This confronts certain liberal visions of human identity as an individualistic existence, and Marxist visions of identity in a purely collectivist sense. In his 1995 encyclical *Ut unum sint* John Paul II described part of the role of dialogue between communities in personalist terminology:

> All dialogue implies a global, existential dimension. It involves the human subject in his or her entirety; dialogue between communities involves in a particular way the subjectivity of each.[19]

The term "personalism" is not necessarily universally used in English language writings concerning CST, though it is often a feature of European work. As a result, it is no surprise that the term itself did not come up in interviews. However, the constituent aspects of it did feature regularly. The idea and language of "dignity" came up consistently across the charities, along with the idea of a deeper understanding of compassion. So while personalism itself may not have been a term used in interviews it here serves as an overview of many themes that were well understood by interviewees.

In regard to our research three particular personalist themes emerged:

1. Finding dignity in everyone
2. Relationships and presence in people's lives
3. Com-passion

1. finding dignity in everyone

A theme that ran through many of the interviews was the importance of viewing everyone as imbued with their own special human dignity. A trustee at Father Hudson's was typical of this trend, saying:

> It defines everything in my work, it is that Matthew 25 idea of looking at people and saying 'you have value in my eyes'. That's what we do; we find the value in people.[20]

This dignity is owed to everyone, even to those who are hard to love. Another interviewee at Father Hudson's made clear that they were very conscious that they worked with people who others might think would be better off not existing, such as "those with dementia, prostitutes, those with disabilities, refugees and asylum seekers, etc." The role of the charity was at least in part, for that interviewee, an exercise in "enshrining the idea that they [those types of people listed above] still have dignity and value".

This commitment was seen as very important in interviews, and not only with staff. The brother of one resident with disabilities spoke of how pleased the family of the resident were that he could live a "full life in his 60s thanks to the help of Father Hudson's... He takes himself to church, he goes to Birmingham FC matches with a carer and overall he's helped to live as independently as possible".

This sense of finding and encouraging dignity in service users is also at the heart of the work of the Apostleship of the Sea. One chaplain discussed the power of being the only visitor to ships who treats all the seafarers "just as humans" and who "doesn't want anything from them". Treating seafarers as real people and trying to bring some aspects of normal everyday existence to them like newspapers and means of communicating with family back home was a critical aspect of what made the AoS so valuable to seafarers.

Tied into that is a particular concern of helping service users to realise their own dignity through self-care, rather than a paternalist attitude of handing out services. In that spirit Father Hudson's home for people living with disabilities, like the other houses and apartments they owned around the area, was designed to allow the residents to be as independent as possible. Obviously that was easier for some than others, but nonetheless there was a consistent focus on letting residents have as much say in their own care as possible. This extended to things like what trips the residents were taken on, what sort of food they were helped to cook for themselves and where they went on holiday. One staff member described how fantastic the holidays were. The residents voted on where they wanted to go, and have so far visited Benidorm and Jersey, staying on sites designed to be disabled friendly.

This focus on self-actualisation defined a number of the different care services provided by Father Hudson's, but was also recognised in other charities. For example, the marriage charities both put significant emphasis on dealing with the issue of self-forgiveness and recognising oneself as worthy of being forgiven as critical in addressing relationship problems.

One of the most interesting examples comes from the experience of the SVP. One trustee and member recalled the discussions over starting the furniture stores:

> When they started I was actually opposed, I didn't think we should be selling things to the poor. But I have come to see the value of people having choice and dignity in being able to choose the things they want and take responsibility for getting them... We were maybe a bit arrogant sometimes in the past [when they gave furniture to people in need] when we just showed up and gave people things. Then a week later you'd see the same stuff dumped, because it wasn't what people actually wanted.

The element of choice, and having the dignity to be able to go to a store and spend money (even at discounted prices), rather than simply being the object of charity was important to people.

2. relationships and presence in people's lives

All six of our charities encouraged a sense of being a presence and ongoing relationship in the lives of their service users. In this they echoed a theme addressed by Benedict XVI who declared that "As a spiritual being, the human creature is defined through interpersonal relationships".[21]

A chaplain at the Apostleship of the Sea went as far as to call it a "sacramental presence". That is to say that their presence on ships embodied the commitment of love to God's people. Implicit in this is a sense of incarnational theology. Just as Jesus became man to manifest the love of God to his people, so the chaplains and visitors of the AoS represent an effort to manifest God's love in their presence and care for seafarers.

A relational presence is the essence of the work of the SVP and their visits to the elderly and poor. Such relationships are only truly effective if they are built over time. Unlike other service providers (like local councils, for example) the SVP do not stop visiting when the immediate crisis is dealt with. The consistency and depth of the relationships is what makes the work effective. Several SVP volunteers shared stories of long-term relationships and seeing whole families change over time, with children who were helped years ago coming back to volunteer or speak to the SVP as adults.

One particularly moving story demonstrated the authenticity that these relationships can have. Two married SVP members had lost a daughter in a road accident. Soon they found they were receiving lots of condolence cards from people they had been visiting, and many of those people also came to the funeral. For the parents this was a remarkable reminder of the authenticity of the friendship they were trying to create:

> The people we thought we were supporting came and supported us... It was a brilliant illustration of the family of the SVP – not just the members but those we help. It is a real friendship relationship.

> *Just as Jesus became man and suffered with humanity so Catholics are called to engage with, and suffer alongside, the poor.*

The importance for care of being able to cultivate relationships was a theme at Father Hudson's too. With many of the services, including the fostering and the adult care, interviewees reiterated the importance of close relationships in being effective. The carer of one service user emphasised how important that was when the service user in question couldn't speak. Since he couldn't verbalise if he was in pain or unhappy, only a carer who had spent real time with him knew how to understand how he felt and how he was communicating. With other services there was no such relationship, mostly due to time and financial restraints.

It was a notable feature of Father Hudson's more broadly that many of the services were individually quite small. This had its downsides but did allow for a bespoke and personal relationship that was highly valued by service users and volunteers. One of the foster carers emphasised how important that was for her; the smallness of the service meant that she knew the staff very well and was able to stay in touch with them and get a lot more support than might otherwise have been the case.

3. Com-passion

The idea of compassion is closely tied to the idea of being a real presence in someone's life, as discussed above. It is an understanding of charity as being beyond just sympathy to something more. One AoS chaplain summarised it most succinctly as the sense that "we do compassion, as in the real meaning of the word; com-passion – suffering with". This again ties into the idea of incarnational theology. Just as Jesus became man and suffered with humanity so Catholics are called to engage with, and suffer alongside, the poor.

> *"It hurts more. That's the truth. When someone dies or goes off the rails it hurts that much more because you actually knew them."*

An SVP member described this in practice as the need to recognise that "it's not enough to give money, real charity is befriending and getting alongside people". There was a recognition that this was difficult. Another SVP interviewee described the cost of being relational and genuinely befriending people was that "it hurts more. That's the truth. When someone dies or goes off the rails it hurts that much more because you actually knew them."

For the marriage charities there was a particular element to compassion which was that all the volunteers (couples who lead the weekends) have to have been on the weekend themselves. They share personal stories of their own marriage troubles and experiences. They are not counsellors but, in the words of one interviewee at Retrouvaille, "wounded healers healing wounded couples". They know what it is to suffer these problems because they have experienced them themselves.

5. family

Support of the family sits in the background to several of the ideas of CST already discussed. The family is understood as the basic unit of society and therefore the first level of subsidiarity, as well as the immediate focus of personal relationships in personalism. The 1997 Rio Declaration on the Family by the Pontifical Council for the Family declared:

> The importance of the family as the basic unit of society has been neglected by many governments and these have failed to undergird it as widespread urbanization, materialistic social trends, practical problems and the social acceptance of selfishness and irresponsibility contribute to the breakdown of families.[22]

As is perhaps to be expected, although all the charities were concerned with projects to support families in some way or another, the two marriage charities stand out for their commitment to talking about family issues. To an extent they saw themselves as counter-cultural forces. In the words of one interviewee at Retrouvaille, "the message from society seems to be that if something isn't working you should give up. Our emphasis is on saying there is always another way out – that divorce isn't the answer."

Of course, such a stance is not without a controversial edge to it. Critics might well question how true it is that all marriages can be redeemed. However, for one thing it ought to be remembered that couples choose to attend these weekends, no one is compelled to do so, and furthermore, while that is the guiding ethos of the charities, they are very clear that they are not counsellors. All the exercises done on the weekends are done by each couple in private. They are not, in other words, directly advised, never mind instructed, on their own particular problems. Such things are left to the couples themselves to work out, or not, as the case may be.

At both marriage charities the particular emphasis on the family, however, was the impact of family beyond the married couple. One aspect of this was the economic and social costs of family breakdown, with the sorts of figures regularly quoted by organisations like Relationships Foundation – who claim marriage breakdown costs the UK economy £48 billion.[23] In a less technical sense, but one with more in common with personalist thinking, this impact was expressed more in terms of the effects on other family members. One interviewee from Retrouvaille, for example, shared that her motivation comes from when:

> ...you see the 20 couples or whatever sitting there and you can also see between them all their kids, extended families, all the other people that this will have an impact on. Some have loads of kids – 9-10 even! You can't help but see that you're touching other generations, that this has an enormous impact on families.

This sense of the importance of keeping in mind a broader family and relational impact than simply the immediate service users was present in several of the charities. A senior staff member at Father Hudson's said:

> We occasionally have it where one of the service users runs out of money and they have to approach us and say "we can no longer afford our share of the care fee, could you just accept the local authority fee?" (i.e. about 50% of the total due). We usually say yes. Makes an enormous difference to that family – we get letters about that. Takes enormous weight off people and lets people be in peace. Have to remember with ageing population now, if we're caring for someone in their 90s then their children are in their 70s – might also be pretty frail. We don't care only for individuals, because they have families and people who love them and if you hurt the individual you hurt the people who love them. That's what Father

Hudson's is about really – it's recognising that human condition and saying that we'll do all we can.

6. evangelisation

In setting out to do this research the previous four major themes (the option for the poor, solidarity, subsidiarity and personalism) were the themes detected from the interviews and broadly corresponded to the expected principles of CST literature. Over the course of the interviews it became clear that a fifth theme of evangelisation made up an additional critical theme that ought to be discussed in its own right. To say that Catholic charities are agents of evangelisation will raise some secular concerns. It taps into a fear, unpacked more thoroughly in Paul Bickley's Theos report *The Problem of Proselytism*, that faith organisations represent an improper or sinister activity looking to take advantage of the vulnerable for the sake of the religious group's own needs.[24]

It should be noted that in the sample of this research none of the Catholic charities researched were what Bickley's report would have classified as "full fat" Faith Based Organisations, i.e. those charities that see participation in a particular religious community as fundamentally part of their service. All of them worked with non-Catholics and, with the exception of the WWME, all of them had non-Catholic volunteers.

Evangelisation nonetheless was a theme of the research and of CST. John Paul II's encyclical *Sollictudo rei socialis* declared that "the teaching and spreading of her social doctrine are part of the Church's evangelising mission".[25] It was a theme to which he returned in a number of encyclicals and sermons and one that has been especially embraced by Pope Francis in *Evangelii gaudium*.[25]

What came out most strongly from the interviews, however, was not evangelisation as a means of reaching out to people outside the Church, so much as the extent to which the charities served as crucibles of spirituality; building the spirituality of those who already considered themselves Catholics. This was recognised in *Deus caritas est* in the idea that love or *caritas* contributes to a "Spirit [which] is the energy which transforms the heart of the ecclesial community so that it becomes a witness before the world to the love of the Father".[26] This transformation of the Church from within was evident in our interviews.

Which is not to say that there was no interest in other people joining the faith, but the expression attributed to St Francis, "preach the gospel, and if you must, use words," ran as a recurring motif through a string of interviews from multiple charities. Examples of preaching without words certainly existed. An interviewee at WWME and another at Father Hudson's both noted the power of charitable work in changing perceptions of the

Church. People were more willing to give it a second chance having benefitted from its services. There was necessary caution over this, not least since Benedict XVI had been quite explicit that charity work cannot be used for "what is nowadays called proselytism".[28]

The evidence of evangelisation of people who were already Catholics, however, was remarkable. Interviewees at WWME noted how far they had changed as a result of the work. Their spirituality had been renewed, and they saw part of their role as "renewing the Church". A similar sense was present in an interview with a trustee from Father Hudson's who said that "we are growing Catholics...all these community projects based out of parishes, they are really motivated, they are bringing people back into the Church".

At the SVP spiritual development is an explicit part of what they do. They have the Vincentian rule[29] and their prayer book to draw on. Several interviewees spoke about how fulfilling the work had been and how their personal faith had grown.

For one of the chaplains at the AoS this is not surprising, but rather is exactly as it should be. The whole point of their work is to renew the personal encounter with Jesus. He reminds his fellow chaplains that they are not "bringing God when we go on board – he's already there". The seafarers encounter something of the love of God in pastoral care offered by a Catholic charity; the chaplains encounter God in those they are serving. It is only natural, therefore, that this work should renew and grow people's faith and spirituality.

This raises the question of whether the Church recognises what it has in its charities in terms of evangelisation. It is easy to see doing good works as a witness that might lead others to the Church. It is perhaps less appreciated how big an impact it can have on the spiritual engagement of lay people who already profess to be Catholics.

chapter one – references

1. Leo XIII *Rerum novarum* (1891) 37
2. Francis *Evangelii Gaudium* (2013) 198
3. http://beta.charitycommission.gov.uk/charity-details/?regid=1053992&subid=0
4. Congregation for the Doctrine of the Faith 'Instruction on Certain Aspects of the "Theology of Liberation"' 1984, available on the Vatican website - http://www.vatican.va/roman_curia/congregations/cfaith/documents/rc_con_cfaith_doc_19840806_theology-liberation_en.html (accessed 11/12/2015).
5. See Paul Bickley *The Problem of Proselytism* (Theos, 2016).
6. John Paul II *Sollicitudo rei socialis* (1987).
7. A good summary of the idea as expressed in British Catholicism is the 1996 statement from the Catholic Bishops' Conference of England and Wales 'The Common Good and the Catholic Church's Social Teaching'.
8. *Compendium of the Social Doctrine of the Church* Pontifical Council for Justice and Peace, 2004) 168.
9. Pope Benedict's letter "On the Service of Charity" (2012) is available on the Vatican website: http://w2.vatican.va/content/benedict-xvi/en/motu_proprio/documents/hf_ben-xvi_motu-proprio_20121111_caritas.html (accessed 11/12/2015).
10. See also Paul Bickley, Good neighbours: *How churches help communities flourish* (Church Urban Fund and Theos 2014) for a summary of these ideas in the context of churches in deprived communities.
11. *Deus caritas est* 26-29.
12. Pius XI, *Quadragesimo anno* (1931) 79.
13. DBS (Disclosure and Barring Service) checks, previously CRB (Criminal Records Bureau) checks, are required to be performed by prospective employers of staff and volunteers working with vulnerable children or adults.
14. According to data from the Internationale Confederation, Society of Saint-Vincent-de-Paul website: http://en.ssvpglobal.org/Global-network/A-international-implantation (accessed 15/12/2015).
15. Emmanuel Mounier (1905-1950) was a French theologian and philosopher who was one of the main intellectual thinkers behind personalism and Christian Democracy in French thought. For an excellent guide see Michael Kelly, *Pioneer of the Catholic Revival: The ideas and influence of Emmanuel Mounier*, (London: Sheed and Ward Ltd, 1979).
16. Jacques Maritain (1882-1973) was a philosopher and theologian who was a major intellectual force behind the early European project, the United Nations and the development of human rights. See John Hittinger, (2002), *Liberty, Wisdom and Grace: Thomism and Democratic Political Theory* (Lanham, MD: Lexington Books, 2002).
17. Leonardo Boff *Trinity and Society* tr. Paul Burns (Orbis Books, 1988).

18   For a summary see Samuel Gregg, *Challenging the Modern World: Karol Wojtyla/John Paul II and the Development of Catholic Social Teaching* (Lexington Books, 2002).

19   John Paul II, *Ut unum sint* (1995) 28.

20   The passage referred to is Matthew 25:38-45 in which Jesus sits in judgement and decalres that "As you did it to one of the least of these my brothers, you did it to me."'.

21   Benedict XVI, *Caritas in Veritate* (2009) 53.

22   Declaration of the Theological Pastoral Congress, World Meeting of the Holy Father with Families, Rio de Janeiro, 4-5 October 1997.

23   Relationships Foundation runs a "Cost of Family Failure Index". The 2016 update put the cost of breakdown at £48 billion. http://www.relationshipsfoundation.org/wp-content/uploads/2016/02/Counting-the-Cost-of-Family-Failure-2016-Update.pdf

24   Paul Bickley, *The Problem of Proselytism*, (Theos, 2015).

25   John Paul II *Sollictudo rei socialis,* (1987) 41.

26   *Evangelii gaudium* (2013).

27   *Deus caritas est* (2005) 16.

28   *Deus caritas est* (2005) 22.

29   For a summary see, for example, *The Rule,* 7th edition, 2012 (amended 2014) issued by the National Council of Australia.

being Catholic today

The first section of this report has looked at the principles of Catholic Social Teaching and the extent to which they are embodied in the work and thinking of Catholic charities. This section moves from looking at principles underpinning charitable work to the more explicit elements of what it means to call yourself "Catholic". To that end it looks at the extent to which the charities have been able to be explicit about their Catholic ethos, what they think that means in practice, the difficulties that such a position can cause and how they relate to the wider Church.

All of our case study charities self-identify as Catholic. However, what that means in terms of how explicit they can be, and where the boundaries are drawn on some issues, varies significantly. Two overarching themes define some of these differences. One is what it means to have a Catholic ethos, and how that is demonstrated in practice. The other is the relationship of the charity to the Church, whether locally, with Catholic networks, with the national hierarchy or even in some cases with Rome.

It is important to note that the official stance of the Church is that charities using the name Catholic must "submit their own Statutes for the approval of the competent ecclesiastical authority [the local bishop]"[1] and are required to comply with a number of requirements detailed in the 2012 *Motu Proprio* letter "On the service of charity". That which has proved to be of particular difficulty is the interpretation of the ruling that charities are "required to follow Catholic principles in their activity and they may not accept commitments which could in any way affect the observance of those principles".[2]

the nature of Catholic ethos

All of the six case study charities identify themselves as Catholic. However, how explicit they are in presenting that ethos either externally (to the general public and secular bodies) or internally (among staff and volunteers) varies. In some other charities the Catholic element of their identity has effectively been muted or abandoned. Adoption charities, often for well-publicised political reasons, have over recent years been especially notable for downplaying or removing Catholic elements of their operations.

It is not uncommon to find charities that once claimed to have a Catholic ethos but have now downgraded that in their literature or on their websites to "Catholic inspired" or to a broader-still "Christian inspired" status. In the opinion of one interviewee this was motivated in large part by fear – especially among charities reliant on public funding – that calling yourself a Catholic charity gave off an image of exclusivity and conservatism and as a result "councils won't touch it".

None of our charities had quite gone so far as to abandon their claim to being Catholic. However, how explicit that was made did certainly vary, sometimes even within charities. Father Hudson's Care is an interesting example. As a charity with a fair amount of public service provision one might have expected, given fears over the potential toxicity of a Catholic identity, that the identity would be most muted there. However, FHC has a chapel in its main building at which a monthly Mass is held for staff who wish to attend. That represents quite a clear piece of expilcit symbolism.

However, other buildings had no such obvious symbolism and it was interesting to note from interviews that staff and volunteers, particularly those based in different buildings and in particular services with the elderly and adults with disabilities, were significantly less conscious of, or concerned by, the Catholic ethos than senior staff had been. This difference in levels is something to which we will return to below.

An interesting dimension of this aspect of how explicit Catholic charities are in expressing their Catholic identity (and that previously stated requirement that charities "follow Catholic principles in their activity and they may not accept commitments which could in any way affect the observance of those principles") is in the marriage charities. In the 1950s, the Catholic Marriage Advisory Council (now called Marriage Care) began receiving government funding as part of a government commitment to legislating in support of family and marriage. Though Marriage Care has never ceased to be clear of its Catholic basis and inspiration it is nonetheless notable that in providing marriage counselling and other services with public money, elements of Catholic teaching and work have tended to be more muted than in the two marriage charities with which we worked. Perhaps because neither WWME nor Retrouvaille received any state funding, both were more explicit in their Catholic identity, most notably in that both involved priests on their weekend retreats, who presented challenges from their own relational ministry. One interviewee at Retrouvaille noted that this had been a real personal challenge for him, as a non-Catholic, to get over. He had not been comfortable when he showed up and saw a priest was there, and it had taken time for him to buy into the process.

Having a priest on the weekends is a very clear external sign to service users of the explicit Catholic basis of the charity. It makes an interesting point of comparison with the SVP, who externally leave the Catholicism fairly implicit (they certainly don't deny it, but many conferences work extensively with people of other faiths or no faith, and don't include any religious element in their visits). Yet there is a very clear sense of an explicit Catholic ethos internally within the organisation. For example, SVP meetings in parishes begin with prayers. Members of the SVP function effectively as a lay order within the broader Vincentian order. That use of prayer as a uniting feature that builds an internal sense of the ethos is something that was also being investigated by Caritas Birmingham, who were looking at creating a prayer resource for their network.

An interesting, if perhaps unsurprising, feature of the interviews was that how explicitly the faith ethos shines through internally in a charity was often seen quite differently at different levels of the organisation (unsurprising, because we would expect in any context the head of an organisation to be more intimately familiar with the strategic aims and purpose of an organisation than staff or volunteers at the other end of the hierarchy). It is worth highlighting though, because it gives an important sense of the difficulty in identifying how Catholic a charity as a whole perceives itself to be.

At Father Hudson's, as was mentioned above, there is a chapel in the main building, and a bishop sits as president of trustees. We might, therefore, assume that the charity has a very explicit Catholic ethos – and to an extent it does. However, that same sense was not present in staff and volunteers in some of the individual services. One, for example, when asked about the religious element of the charity, responded that "you don't really notice it. It's there if you want it, but to be honest it's not obvious". When volunteers and service users were asked about the ethos of the charity, overwhelmingly they answered that it was about high quality care for those in need, but relatively few brought up any religious element to that without prompting, and when prompted, few had a sense of what it meant beyond a historic allegiance.

This sense of the Catholic ethos being more apparent at some levels of organisations than others was a feature of a number of interviews. Of course, it also has a legal dimension when it comes to employment law. Not all of our charities had any staff at all but those that did all had some roles in which being a Catholic was an occupational requirement (such as the paid chaplaincy roles of the AoS and the Chief Executives of the AoS and SVP among others) and other roles which had no such requirement (such as the professional caring staff at the FHC or some of the national office roles at the SVP). All staff hired at the FHC are made aware of the Catholic ethos and history of the charity, but there is no expectation that Catholic faith is necessary in all roles.

None of this is to say that there were not volunteers and staff at all levels of the charities who were absolutely conscious of, and keen to promote the charity's Catholic ethos, only that the extent to which is was embedded did seem to decline further down organisations.

A final key point on the issue of ethos is a consideration of the difficulties of apparent clashes between that ethos and other concerns. In particular, this possible difficulty manifests itself in areas where there is a particular tension over Catholic teaching, such as homosexuality, divorce, contraception and working with other faiths. It should be made clear that these were not necessarily problematic, but that there were potential pressures and concerns here which either made some charities come to particular compromises over their Catholic status or else was recognised as, sometimes, a difficult public perception to overcome.

Homosexuality is an interesting case in point. The Catholic Church's difficulties in responding to homosexuality are well known. One gay employee at Father Hudson's noted that it being a Catholic charity had initially worried him before he applied for the role. In fact, he had found the atmosphere incredibly supportive and welcoming, and rather better than several other workplaces he had been in. Yet the fact that he hesitated before applying is symptomatic of a common worry – that "Catholic" is potentially incompatible with the identity of gay staff or service users. Of course, this reached a particular peak in the much-publicised disputes over Catholic adoption agencies. In practice a number of such agencies either split from the Catholic Church or significantly muted their Catholic identity. In the case of the adoption agency that had once been part of Father Hudson's it split off to become a separate charity with a different and more arm's length relationship with the Church than its previous status had been.

Of course, for the marriage charities there are a number of areas of potential clash on this issue. At present WWME has not had a gay couple seek help, though branches of their charities in other countries had been approached, in one or two cases accompanied with legal challenges. Retrouvaille is clear in its commitment to heterosexual married couples though they have had a transgender couple approach them to attend a programme. They do not currently offer their programme to same sex couples. WWME have traditionally reiterated that they work within the Catholic conception of marriage and at least one interviewee wondered, with that in mind and the availability of marriage counsellors in other settings, how likely the situation really is to arise. Interviewees at WWME not quite sure what they would do if they were approached by a gay couple.

In a sense it mirrored debates that they had experienced, in which couples who were unmarried, divorced or had a civic marriage but not a Catholic one had approached them. In each of these cases they were being approached by couples who did not strictly fit the criteria of a Catholic marriage. Interviewees at WWME said that they would be very happy to take any such couple, including a gay couple, on the weekend so long as, in the words of one interviewee "they were clear where we were coming from... We don't want to be judgemental and we want to help whoever needs help, but we are going to talk from a

Catholic perspective and wouldn't want to change that". Another simply said "we never apologise for it being a Catholic marriage encounter".

For WWME, which has seen international partners take quite different approaches to some of these questions, with some having dropped their Catholic identity entirely for fear of it being seen as too exclusivist or judgemental, and others having reinforced their Catholic status, this was a live question without a clear solution. It had a dimension in terms of finding volunteers too. WWME volunteer couples are expected to be Catholics, but with fewer and fewer couples coming through where both of them were Catholic this was becoming increasingly difficult to maintain.

This worry on the part of secular bodies that Catholic charities will not work with outsiders should in some ways be considered odd. The official stance of the Church as laid out in Benedict XVI's encyclical *Deus caritas est* is explicit that charitable activity cannot be used "for proselytism" and that "love is free".[3] Nonetheless it was a worry that was consistently mentioned, raising the question of why it is that Catholic charities (or perhaps faith bodies more broadly) have managed to gain this reputation.

relationship with the Church

The preceding section dealt with the questions of what it is to embody a Catholic ethos. What follows is the question of how our charities practically relate to the wider Catholic Church.

One question here was the extent to which relationships with the Church are a help or a hindrance to charities. Certainly there were plenty of examples of helpfulness. At the local level there is often a reliance on parishes to provide premises and a local volunteer base. The community projects at Father Hudson's, for example, often operate out of parish centres. Similarly the SVP, which generally functions on a parish level, often relies on the local parish church to provide a venue for any services it might provide.

Being a local charity with a close relationship to a parish church tends to open up a charity to a wider volunteer and funding base. Interviewees from the SVP, AoS and WWME all recalled how they first got involved in volunteering when someone from their parish gave an announcement in church about the work of the charity. For the SVP, the local church also frequently operates as the means by which service users find out about the charity, or where SVP members find out about people who need help. One SVP interviewee noted that "really there's no point where SVP work ends and normal life begins." They frequently were involved in talking to people from the parish and weren't quite sure whether to count that as SVP work or something else.

The funding relationship between Church and Catholic charities is often a close one. The AoS, for example, is funded largely through the annual Sea Sunday collection in Catholic churches and schools. Father Hudson's also relies extensively on giving from Catholic churches and schools in the Birmingham Archdiocese.

At a broader level there are various networks that exist to support Catholic charities. Caritas Birmingham of course actually is, itself, a network designed to support smaller projects and one set up as part of the broader Caritas effort and with the enthusiastic support of the local Archbishop. For others, CSAN (Caritas Social Action Network) functions as the overall social action arm of the Catholic Church in England and Wales. It operates as a network with four departments (homelessness, older people, children and families, and vulnerable adults) providing various resources for member charities.

These resources were generally welcomed by those of our charities that were members (the two marriage charities are not members). It was noted by one senior management figure that CSAN mirrors the issues in several of its members in defining how "Catholic" it really is, and how far it expects its members to embody a Catholic ethos. There was also a specific issue for the AoS, who are keen to contribute to CSAN but, partly because they operate in a slightly unusual field of social action, don't seem to fit easily into any of the available categories (a struggle they also have as part of the Catholic Bishops, Conference of England and Wales CBCEW, where they sit in international affairs). These issues aside, CSAN and Caritas respectively provide useful networks and resources for Catholic charities, and are closely tied into the hierarchy of the Church.

The two marriage charities are not part of CSAN (though WWME did attempt to join at one point). This presented a difficulty for WWME because without a recognised network with which to work it was proving more difficult to have shared resources and to gain the support of the Church. They had had some success working with marriage and family life officers in some dioceses, but far more limited success (and no little frustration) in cultivating relationships with bishops. Retrouvaille, which by contast currently works only in the dioceses of Westminster and Plymouth, noted that they had had excellent relationships with the relevant bishops.

The role of networks, and of bishops, accordingly functions as something of a double edged sword. Where the networks exist there were glowing reports of the work of the Church as a supportive advocate of its charities. Father Hudson's has the Archbishop of Birmingham as president of trustees and enjoys an excellent relationship with the diocese, while the AoS has a Bishop Promoter in the Catholic Bishops Conference. Where, however, networks have broken down or do not exist it can be difficult for small charities to have access to the advantages enjoyed by Catholic charities in other sectors. In fact frustration was high, with one WWME interviewee admitting that when it came to trying to communicate with the Church "we've given up".

Nor was this necessarily the only way in which relationships with the Church could prove to be a hindrance as much as a help. A complaint voiced in several charities was the issue of territorial behaviour. For example, one interviewee from an SVP group noted that there had been difficulties with a local parish priest who did not want an SVP group operating in his parish. His rationale was that he had too few parishioners willing to volunteer and help with things and that he was worried that the SVP would "steal" all the available volunteers. While it should be noted that generally SVP volunteers had nothing but praise for their parish priest and their relationships with him, this was not an entirely isolated occurrence. An interviewee at WWME remembered a similar experience, when their own parish priest had been reluctant to support the charity and her role within in.

This was also highlighted by interviews at Caritas Birmingham:

> The biggest challenge to subsidiarity is when you get tired priests.... They do a lot and eventually it wears them down, and we have no other priests to replace them, so you get stagnation, they don't want to hear about local projects or anything else.

The same interviewee went on to say "the Church has been very poor at empowering lay leadership. For too long it has tried to keep this sort of thing as a clergy-led in-house process." This was a part of a wider issue. Charities are increasingly growing in distance from formal governance relationships with the Church and are becoming less reliant on the Church for funding and leadership than they once were. This is not so much a conscious choice as a necessity given increasing financial restraints and a lack of priests. An interviewee at FHC believed that this move was in part driven by the decline of the religious orders, who would have once done much of the social action work which is now done almost exclusively by the laity.

This struggle to empower lay leadership or to have real clarity on the differing functions of laity and clergy is one which can be detected in CST documents. Pope Benedict XVI's *Deus caritas est* is devoted to being a thorough outworking of Catholic teaching on charity, yet makes notably little mention of the exact function of the laity. In fact the clearest sense of the differentiation of roles comes in the form of a historical survey of the development of the Church and the formation of the *diaconia* to perform this charitable function.[4] Moving beyond the early Church to modern times might have been more helpful in fully defining the differentiation of roles.

To some extent the Church and Catholic charities operate in an inevitable symbiosis – what affects one, will affect the other. Yet the relationship seems in some respects to be shifting. Charities are becoming less reliant on the Church even as the Church becomes ever more reliant on charities to fulfil social action and, as was noted above, even to do evangelisation.

The symbiosis is evident when you see some of the challenges facing particular charities. The decline (at least outside of London) in the numbers of people attending church each week, the ageing profile of those who do, and the loosening of Church control over its faith schools has in practice had a significant effect on charities. The SVP, AoS and WWME have all experienced difficulties in attracting volunteers (though it has varied significantly in extent from place to place). Once they would have relied on parishes to provide a pool of volunteers, but today that pool is much smaller, as is the funding that comes from second collections.

The symbiotic effect is seen in other respects too. At the negative end of the spectrum the spectre of the sex abuse scandal had had a knock-on effect on the popularity of Catholic charities. At the positive end several interviewees at different charities noted the boost that they had received from the Pope Francis effect. What Catholic charities do will also have an impact on perceptions of the Church. Success stories help counter negative narratives, but problems like another sex abuse scandal at a charity would tarnish the Church (no matter how much the charity in question was embodying a Catholic ethos).

chapter 2 – references

1   On the Service of Charity *Motu Proprio* 2012
2   *ibid*
3   *Deus caritas est* (2005) 22.
4   *Deus caritas est* (2005) 17.

3

the challenges facing Catholic charities

The final section of this report looks at what factors provide the most significant challenges to Catholic charities. Some of these have already been identified in the previous sections of the report, particularly in relation to challenges that stem from living out a distinctive Catholic ethos. However, this section is designed to provide an overview of all the areas identified in interviews as being a limiting factor on the work of these charities (although some will not be exclusive to Catholic charities, but might be equally applicable to any charity). These challenges have been grouped into three themes: practical/political challenges, religious challenges and intellectual challenges.

practical/political

This group of challenges represent in some ways the most immediate and obvious ones – those things that make it difficult to practically provide charitable activity. Some of them are the result of government policy, others more basically practical, such as difficulties in finding volunteers.

austerity and the increasing scope of the need

Those charities working particularly in traditional social action work such as confronting homelessness, disability, poverty and isolation among the elderly were all extremely concerned at a trend that saw them having to meet more needs than ever, with less and less public financial support. How this was phrased ranged from significant wariness, such as from one interviewee at Caritas Birmingham who said:

> We have to respect that government has a really difficult job, and it isn't fair to my mind to think that some of the consequences of particular policies are deliberate. But, I have to say we are seeing more needs coming up and there is no doubt that there is less local government money about to help.

all the way to significantly more angry reflections on austerity politics including from one senior figure at a charity who declared,

There is no doubt that this government are targeting some of the most vulnerable in making their savings.

In practical terms, one senior staff member at Father Hudson's Care summed up the effect of austerity as simply being that it

> can really drain you when cuts come and there is less money available. This year [2015] has been the worst in a decade for local authority support – if we weren't doing it no one would be in this area.

Several other staff members from different charities echoed similar stories – that local services supporting vulnerable people were seriously underfunded. Several SVP members reflected bleakly that they were dreading the effects of the coming winter.

The staff who worked with the elderly at Father Hudson's Care noted that their role is in some ways becoming more difficult as an indirect consequence of funding cuts. Because the council is only prepared to meet care costs for more extreme cases than was previously the case, people are coming to the home much later in life, in correspondingly worse health and often with more complex care needs (particularly around dementia). One simply said "just sustaining the current standards with so much less money coming in from the council is going to be almost impossible". A senior member of staff mentioned a particular social justice element to that equation – they could charge more from the elderly themselves, but if they did so they would effectively price out the poor most in need of help.

Just sustaining the current standards with so much less money coming in from the council is going to be almost impossible.

Naturally this was a particular challenge for those charities in receipt of public funding. However, there was a knock-on effect for others too – including in seeing an increased strain on alternative funding providers (notably the Church) and in terms of an increasing need to step in and support people with services previously provided by the state. One example is the increasing work the SVP is doing in some conferences in helping people to fill in forms online. The benefits system has overwhelmingly now moved online, but for many people that makes it very difficult for them to access, understand or complete the forms needed for them to get the money to which they are entitled. Job centres were criticised for not understanding or helping sufficiently with those needs – hence the increased need for the SVP. Many SVP conferences have felt the need to start or contribute towards foodbanks, particularly to serve those service users whose payments had been delayed by bureaucratic problems.

There was, for the SVP, one bright side to the increasing scope of activities they were expected to cover due to austerity; relationships with many local authorities had improved significantly. One senior member of staff at the SVP noted that in the past there had often been tensions with local government, especially those more minded to secular charities and resisting religious service providers. Her observation was that in the current financial climate those concerns had been largely abandoned, since local authorities were, in her words, "far more desperate for help wherever it can be found". Naturally that raises the question of how permanent such a rapprochement really is, and also whether Christians ought to be worried about being tolerated only if they are expected to provide services that, arguably, ought really to be state-provided.

There was also a legitimate concern about how far it was within their remit to criticise government. Part of this was down to fears over the new lobbying act and what that meant for campaigning.[1] Another aspect was a fear of falling foul of Church policy on these issues. The papal encyclical that most explicitly deals with charities, *Deus caritas est* devotes significant length to the idea that the responsibility for creating a "just society" belongs to the political realm – a different space from the space of charity.[2] No interviewee explicitly mentioned this encyclical – but the sense that the Church was not keen on charities directly politically intervening was present in several interviews.

volunteers, funding and symbiosis with the wider Church

Among the most pressing concerns for a number of charities was a difficulty in finding sufficient volunteers and funding. Often, though not always, this was tied to wider issues in the Church.

The AoS was typical of a number of charities that had a concern over finding new volunteers to serve as ship visitors. Their volunteer base was becoming quite elderly in some areas. This was tied, staff suspected, to the fact that congregations in many parts of the country are shrinking and becoming older. This reduces the available Catholic volunteer base. That was also a concern for several other charities. A strategic level interviewee at the SVP noted that recruitment at the SVP was steady, but that that had required a huge amount of effort and a significant recruitment drive.

Inevitably it was easier to find volunteers in some areas than others. In traditional Catholic areas in the North of England the charity tends to be quite strong, while it has a far more minimal presence in other areas. In less Catholic areas a big challenge has been the grouping of churches into ever larger parishes, forcing people to travel significantly further to attend meetings and creating far larger areas for them to be responsible for.

In this the symbiosis between trends in the Catholic Church and Catholic charities becomes clear. Volunteers and funding from traditional sources in parishes are becoming ever more difficult to secure. This is all the more the case when the austerity issues mentioned above mean that churches are often called upon financially and otherwise to support more and more local charities and work. This raises the spectre of what interviewee saw as "compassion fatigue" in which churches were strained beyond their ability to care or relate to the vast number of issues being brought before them. For a senior interviewee at Caritas Birmingham priests are particularly relevant in this. There are too few priests and those that there are are often increasingly elderly and overstretched. They are frankly, for this interviewee, "too tired, and it's a big barrier in practice to subsidiarity".

Finding volunteer couples was also a problem for WWME, partly for similar reasons as already stated, partly due to a decline in marriages featuring two Catholic partners (as opposed to mixed marriages), and partly due to a difficulty in sustaining demand for services. WWME has always drawn the volunteer couples who run the weekend retreats from those couples who have themselves been through the programme. WWME has in recent times struggled to maintain the popularity of those weekends and so the pool of people who might become volunteers has correspondingly shrunk.

The greater issue there of course is why demand is declining. It is notable that there remains significant demand for their services in providing marriage preparation, but not marriage encounter (the service for enriching and supporting existing marriages). Various factors were suggested as possibly coming into play, including the observation that there are simply fewer marriages and married couples in church on any given Sunday to hear about the service. The growth of the marriage counselling industry and perhaps changing social attitudes towards marriage as an institution were also suggested as possible factors. Overall it was not clear what the real driving force behind the decline might be, certainly not to stakeholders. The nature of being an organization without paid staff meant there was a lack of time and resources to understand why that might be and take steps to avert it.

buildings and resources

At the most basic practical level, charities often struggle to get hold of the resources needed to be effective. Most notable in this are premises and spaces with several of our charities in practice being reliant on being given free or heavily subsidised space in parish centres and churches and staff. The issue of physical space is an interesting one. The AoS have tried to move away from seafarers' centres (buildings in ports usually with some entertainment and communication facilities for seafarers) on the basis that they are not really what seafarers want. Instead they have endeavoured to get onto ships and speak to as many people as possible there.

By contrast other charities need some physical space to function effectively. Some of the community projects supported by Father Hudson's Care and/or Caritas Birmingham rely on using space given to them, or else subsidised by local churches. Things like foodbanks, meeting spaces for SVP groups, jobs clubs and other services need spaces and there are often few to be found. Several of the FHC projects were crammed into spaces in parish centres without which they would not have been able to operate. Once again, this reveals something of the symbiotic relationship of Church and charity – the Church is providing a large amount of space which would otherwise have been a problematic expense for many charities.

The other key resource issue is one of staffing. The two marriage charities and Caritas Birmingham had no paid staff at all. AoS and SVP had relatively small London-based national offices which provided things like legal, accounting and media work (among other things) that are best co-ordinated at a national level. FHC has the most paid staff, particularly working in adult care or in the various professional services. The community projects it supports have a more significant range in the ratio of paid staff to volunteers.

In practice this leads to two sets of challenges. For charities reliant on volunteers for their leadership there is a corresponding difficulty in having the time and expertise to respond to all the issues that may arise. A complaint of all three charities with no paid staff was that there just wasn't enough time to commit to do all the necessary work.

On the flip side for charities with paid staff one challenge is of embedding the ethos. There was something of a drop-off in the commitment of paid staff to the Catholic ethos in some charities versus that present in the trustees or among some volunteers. Paid staff rarely had an occupational requirement to be Catholic. The other challenge is being seen to have the right balance in terms of how a charity's funds are spent. For FHC having paid professional staff in many areas is a necessity. Work with adults with disabilities, for example, requires training, safeguarding and expertise over and above what most entirely voluntary organisations are able to provide.

However, for a charity like the SVP whose funding largely comes from congregations there is a concern to be seen as far as possible to be spending donations directly on the care work that people think they are funding. In a climate in which charities are often criticised for spending excessive sums on executive pay and not enough on their charitable activity this is very much a live concern. That being said, a certain number of staff members are required simply to keep the charity going. Finding a balance here is a real difficulty.

publicity, particularly outside the Church

A consistent theme across all six charities was that they were often quite well-known in Catholic circles, but struggled to have any public profile beyond Catholics. The SVP is a good example: despite working with tens of thousands of service users and having some 8,000 volunteer members there was a recognition that the charity was simply not very well known among non-Catholics. A lot of the work in fundraising and advertising services for all of the charities in question was done through the Catholic press or in Catholic churches, with less attention being spent on other areas.

Of course having a high profile within the Church is beneficial, and not to be underestimated, especially if it helps with the charity's ethos or is the source for funding and volunteers. However, having a wider public profile is a growing necessity given some of what has been argued above about the problems of parish decline and ageing congregations. Without a wider base from which to attract volunteers and supporters it will become increasingly difficult for charities to have a stable future.

There is also an aspect of this which is relevant in terms of the evangelisation discussed in the first part of this report. If charities represent something of a soft entry point in religion and spirituality for those who are either detached from the Church of else call themselves Catholic but do not regularly attend Mass then charities and the Church need to find a way of reaching out and appealing to such people. The means of doing so will likely be different to the way in which charities have traditionally operated.

The need to raise publicity outside the Church was something that was recognised by the charities, and they were taking steps to address the issue. More than one had recently created new staff roles designed to meet precisely that need. How that situation develops will be critical to many Catholic charities.

funding pressures

Aside from the points already made about the difficulties with austerity and declining congregations another funding issue is the way a system has developed that demands constant expansion. There is a particular difficulty, recognised by fundraisers at several charities, in finding funding for pre-existing projects and salaries. By contrast, it is relatively easy to find money for new projects and roles.

In practice this has led to several charities and community projects being in the precarious position of requiring constant expansion. In order to fund existing work and salaries it is necessary to think up new projects and ideas and find funding for those. This cycle of constant applications and spreading into new projects was very worrying for some projects who had concerns over the long-term sustainability of such organisation. Already there was a degree of instability in a number of places. One community project associated with Father Hudson's Care had just received a big piece of funding that supported three staff members. Had that particular application not come off in all likelihood it would have been impossible to retain those three roles and the project would have severely struggled to keep their current level of activity going.

religious challenges

The challenges of "being Catholic" and of the difficulties that can emerge in relations with the Church have largely been covered in the previous part of this report. They generally revolve around difficulties in reconciling a Catholic ethos with other views on issues like abortion, divorce, homosexuality and sexual ethics, or else on relationships with the Church – which can serve as either a significant help or else a sometime barrier to charities.

Leaving those issues aside as having been covered in some depth above, this section will focus on a few other areas in which there are religious challenges that hold charities back.

empowering lay leadership

Catholic charities, particularly, but not only, those with a looser Catholic ethos tend to be run by and for lay people. Though several of our charities did have clergy involved either as trustees or in the practical work (the AoS has several Catholic priests serving as chaplains, though other chaplains are lay people, WWME and Retrouvaille both have priests who play a major role on their retreats) they are all designed with some deliberate distance from clerical hierarchical structures. This level of independence from the Church was seen as important, but does then require lay leadership.

That in and of itself is not a challenge except that, for one trustee of Caritas Birmingham this has been a great weakness of the Church. "We need a much better effort at working out what the Church means by subsidiarity in practice... the Church has been quite poor at empowering lay leadership." For him, seeing the work of Caritas Birmingham as empowering local projects and charities one of the difficulties has been moving people past the point where they see everything as having to have a priest lead it.

The hope for Caritas Birmingham is to see far more projects run and managed entirely by lay people, but that hasn't always been easy. The model of Church and of Catholic charity that they are hoping to see is based on the gospel idea of Jesus' commission to the apostles to go out[3] and do practical work.[4] A trustee at FHC recognised that intent, but shared a concern that the Church hasn't done enough to encourage lay leadership, or even the more basic assumption that "you have to *do* something, not just go to church each week!"

secular pressures

There was mixed testimony on whether being a religious charity had held back charities or had been a problem in dealing with secular bodies. Some SVP groups had certainly experienced that, at least in the past – though as above in the note on austerity it was the sense of some senior staff that this was no longer as much of a problem in the current financial climate. Those who worked in the SVP shops in Leeds said that they reported to the local council, but had never had any problems with them since starting up. This was echoed by an interviewee at Caritas Birmingham who noted that generally secular bodies had been very positive so long as they made it clear they were happy to work with everyone.

Others, though, remained concerned, and felt the burden on them to prove their good intentions was disproportionately high,[5] one for example said that it was clear that "Roman Catholic Church is not fashionable, we have to keep showing that our motivation is pure, that we're not all child abusers, that we are prepared to work with everyone. They want us to defend everything twice as hard as anyone else."

Obviously pressures with secular bodies will be more relevant to those charities working with public services and/or in receipt of public funds. Many charities simply won't be in that bracket and so their relationship with secular bodies is unlikely to be a great concern. For those who do work in those areas the evidence of our interviews was mixed, though there was an acknowledgment that Christian charities were expected to jump through quite a few hoops to meet public criteria. This finding is also familiar from other work in the area.[6] Most of our interviewees who acknowledged that issue were not angry or resentful of this, so much as just accepting that this was the way of things for religious bodies in British public life.

ecumenism

A final religious challenge is the ability of Catholic charities to relate not to secular organisations but to organisations from other faith groups. There was an acknowledgement from a number of interviewees that sometimes being a Catholic charity lends itself to thinking only in terms of Catholicism and accordingly doing less work with other groups than might be sensible. A senior interviewee at the AoS admitted this was a danger because, particularly on work like advocacy and speaking up for seafarers' rights, "it can be a weakness, and can be a bit thinking in silos, when we know there are other charities in the area we could talk to and have a louder voice together".

There are, of course, a number of factors to consider in working with other faiths, not least issues of how compatible their respective ethoses actually are. The AoS acknowledged the place for working together on advocacy, but were less enthusiastic about sharing the pastoral work. Some chaplains had had negative experiences working with charities from other faiths in the area and one talked about a "lack of respect for difference on their part – particularly when it comes to the importance to Catholic seafarers of Catholic sacraments".

This then is a question for Catholic charities in the future – how best and most appropriately to work with groups from other faiths without compromising their own Catholic identity.

intellectual challenges

By "intellectual challenges" what is meant is those challenges that are not necessarily immediate dangers or practical hurdles to overcome, but rather are issues that require further consideration and long-term efforts to confront.

dealing with perceptions and history

The spectre of the Catholic sex abuse scandal continues to haunt Catholic charities. Several interviewees recalled experiences when they had been challenged with the scandal and the Church's record and the basic idea that Catholics cannot be trusted with the vulnerable. More broadly still, and reflecting that symbiotic relationship with the Church there was often a challenge of overcoming perceptions of what the Church either teaches or else is perceived to teach.

So, for example, several charities which worked with clients of any faith or none regularly reported that that surprised people who had assumed that it was only for Catholics, or that a judgemental attitude would prevent the charity working with certain sorts of service user.

This need not necessarily be negative. Other interviewees noted how often people sought out their particular charity on the basis that there was an assumption that with Catholic charities came a certain guaranteed level of Christian care and concern. A service user at Father Hudson's was typical of that trend. He noted that he had not particularly cared about what the faith background of the charity was when his relative had first gone there, but that subsequently he had come to feel that "there was something different about the place – hard to identity – but a sort of different sense of purpose, that I guess could well be something to do with their faith". He went on to say that "if they stopped being a faith based charity I think I would want to know the reason for that, and what about it would be different."

Another positive is that the symbiotic relationship between Church and charity can lead to changes of perception led by the Church. The "Pope Francis effect"[7] may be difficult to accurately chart in terms of people going to church but it certainly seemed to have had an impact on charities, with a range of interviewees reporting how much more positively they felt they had been received since Francis became Pope. It had also had a rejuvenating effect on some volunteers and staff – an SVP volunteer spoke for many when she said that she felt that the Pope's vision of service and compassion really spoke to her on a personal level: "he's my type of Pope… the others were too theological and academic for me".

professionalism

There can be a difficult balancing act for charities on professionalism. On the one hand there is the danger (and sometimes legitimate criticism) of being seen as mere "do-gooders" and amateurs who lack the professional skills or competence of non-charity workers. Conversely, there is also the danger of, in a sense, over-professionalising and becoming another clinical type of care that abandons the personal and caring touch that is embodied in a Catholic ethos.

How charities negotiate that balance varies. The two marriage charities, for example, are very explicit that they are not marriage counsellors. They do not claim to be any better or necessarily more effective than, or even an alternative to, marriage counsellors – only that they are a different model of care. SVP volunteers and AoS chaplains are also explicit that they are not professional counsellors – though both receive training and might share certain techniques in common with counsellors.

To a degree that level of difference is a deliberate and important one. An interviewee at Retrouvaille, for example, noted that there is certainly no shortage of counselling services available and that as a result those that choose their services are actively after something a bit different.

Of course, at the other end of the spectrum there needs to be a level of professional accountability, particularly when working with vulnerable people. That process is not always easy. The SVP had lost some and annoyed other members when it insisted that all volunteers had to be DBS checked[8] regardless of how long they had been volunteers. For some who had been in the society for a long time this was perceived as an insult and an unnecessary bureaucratic intervention. For the charity as a whole it was part of an important effort to maintain a degree of professional and safeguarding standards that would protect vulnerable people and also the charity itself from safeguarding problems.

chapter 3 – references

1. The full title is 'The Transparency of Lobbying, Non-party Campaigning and Trade Union Administration Act 2014' which placed significant limits on the abilities of charities to campaign on political issues in the run up to elections. A report by the Commission on Civil Society and Democratic Engagement, *Non-party political campaigning ahead of elections* (2015), found that the act placed significant restrictions on charities and caused significant costs and confusion.
2. *Deus caritas est* (2005) 20-25.
3. Matthew 28: 18-20.
4. Matthew 10: 5-13.
5. See, for example, Bickley. *Problem of Proselytism,* (2015).
6. Ibid, and also *Religion or belief in the workplace and service delivery: Findings from a call for evidence* report from the Equality and Human Rights Commission 2015.
7. The supposed public effect of Pope Francis in improving perceptions of the Church both internally and externally which has been explored by a number of journalists and reports including John Gehring, *The Francis Effect: A Radical Pope's Challenge to the American Catholic Church,* (Rowan and Littlefield, 2015 and 'The Francis Effect: The pope as a turnaround CEO' *The Economist 19* April 2014.

conclusion

There has been a sense throughout this research that the questions raised about the place of Catholic charities and their ethos and identity are of growing importance. For the Church Catholic charities, quite apart from performing the basic Christian commission to go out and do good works (a "constitutive element of the Church's mission and an indispensable expression of her very being"[1]), are increasingly serving as the primary locus of Christian involvement in public life. Given the declining sizes of congregations (at least outside London), the shortage of priests and the struggles of the religious orders and pressures on faith schools, Catholic charities increasingly are becoming the main representatives of the Church.

> *Catholic charities increasingly are becoming the main representatives of the Church.*

This is a necessary role, for as Pope Benedict reminded the Church in 2005 "the Church cannot neglect the service of charity any more than she can neglect the Sacraments and the Word."[2]

Not only that, but as this report has argued, Catholic charities serve as crucibles of evangelisation – providing a space in which Catholic spirituality is grown and expressed. Charities do not necessarily do much to evangelise to non-Catholics, but certainly have a profound impact on growing the faith within Catholic staff and volunteers.

How the Church, therefore, thinks through its relations with its charities is going to be a critical question. For charities, too, there is the issue of how to be Catholic and what it means to have a religious ethos in a public square that at times seems resolutely secular. The Church and Catholic charities need each other – their relationship is symbiotic.

With that in mind the evidence on CST should give cause for optimism, and offer space for significantly more interaction. Certainly there is evidence of Catholic charities genuinely embodying the themes of the option for the poor, solidarity, subsidiarity, personalism, and evangelisation in innovative and powerful ways. There is also, however, a gap between some of the depth of content behind those ideas in CST and how they are actually understood in practice. The option for the poor and solidarity (along with other ideas from CST like the common good and human dignity) were terms and themes that arose regularly in interviews without prompting, though the degree to which they were really understood varied significantly. Other principles, notably subsidiarity, were often evident in practice, but were not terms that were used or at least understood except by a minority of interviewees.

There is space for more dialogue and teaching on the part of the Church to bridge that knowledge gap and provide its charities with more intellectual and spiritual resources to underpin their work.

Equally there is significant space for the Church and academia to learn something from the practical experiences of charities and their work to embody these big principles into British society. This is not a new observation, indeed Pope Paul VI in 1971 summarised a similar idea:

> It is with all its dynamism that the social teaching of the Church accompanies men in their search. If it does not intervene to authenticate a given structure or to propose a ready-made model, it does not thereby limit itself to recalling general principles. It develops through reflection applied to the changing situations of this world, under the driving force of the Gospel as the source of renewal when its message is accepted in its totality and with all its demands.[3]

This, then, is a symbiotic relationship which has challenges, both in terms of realising the principles of Catholic Social Teaching and in a host of other practical, religious and intellectual challenges, not all of which are unique to Catholic charities. It is also one of opportunity – for the Church to see the way CST can be used and the Catholic faith embedded in society, and for charities to gain the intellectual and spiritual (as well as practical) support of the Church to fulfil their work.

conclusion – references

1 *Deus caritas est,* (2005) p. 25.
2 *Deus caritas est,* (2005) p. 17.
3 Paul VI's *Octagosima adveniens (1971).*